IMAGES OF ENGLAND

CALAMITY CORNER

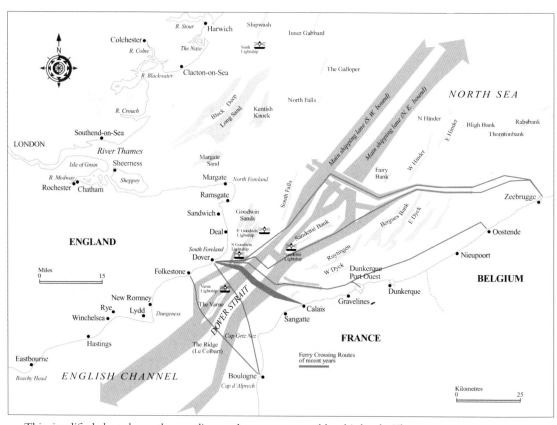

This simplified chart shows the coastlines and sea area covered by this book. The numerous sandbanks indicate the difficulties of navigating the Thames Estuary and eastern English Channel. Large ships must follow the carefully marked channels or they face a grave risk of running aground. Routes through the Channel separation zone are highlighted as they are the busiest, but there is also a major flow of shipping in and out of the Thames and Felixstowe on one side and the ports of Dunkirk and Zeebrugge on the other.

IMAGES OF ENGLAND

CALAMITY CORNER

ANTHONY LANE

TEMPUS

Dedication

To all who suffered, survived or succumbed in the battles with or on the Narrow Seas, this book is respectfully dedicated.

This nation has been challenged more than once,
When the enemy approached, they manned the guns,
For England's tempting shores lay close a'lee,
After those fights were o'er, blood stained the sea.

Such battles were won and others lost,
Ships born on seas once calm became tempest tossed,
Some were saved, others broken on a cruel strand,
Their crews drowned or eternally grateful to reach land.

Ships that nowadays lawfully pass by night or day,
Through these Narrow Seas must carefully make their way,
Lest a violent collision occur and fire prevail,
With dire result and a woeful tale,

For this was once Calamity Corner!

First published 2004

Tempus Publishing Limited
The Mill, Brimscombe Port,
Stroud, Gloucestershire, GL5 2QG
www.tempus-publishing.com

British Library Cataloguing in Publication Data.
A catalogue record for this book is available from the British Library.

ISBN 0 7524 3163 3

Typesetting and origination by Tempus Publishing Limited.
Printed in Great Britain by Midway Colour Print, Wiltshire.

Contents

	Acknowledgements	6
	Introduction	7
one	Warship Casualties	13
two	Mercantile Victims of War	43
three	A Saga of Collisions	63
four	Ships Ashore	83
five	Fires Aboard Ship	121
six	The Rescuers, the Price and the Prizes	129
	Index	157

Acknowledgements

A considerable number of people have helped in the research and preparation of this book, either by providing photographs or supplying information. Among those who have made the greatest contributions are Michael Hunt of the Ramsgate Maritime Museum, Bob Bradley of the Margate Museum and various staff members both past and present of the Deal and Dover Museums. To those institutions and their representatives I extend my sincere thanks.

While every attempt has been made to identify and indicate the origin of as many of the pictures as possible, in some cases it is particularly difficult to trace the original photographer or artist. Among those who have helped me particularly in locating pictures are the late John G. Callis, Mike Jackson, Chris Fright and particularly Philip Neumann of Fotoflite, whose firm has taken so many dramatic pictures of wrecks over the years. Tony Smith, archivist of the World Ship Society, has been extremely kind in providing pictures of ships in service before they were unfortunate enough to be wrecked.

I acknowledge a great debt to two publications originating from the Royal National Lifeboat Institution (RNLI): Supplements to their annual reports giving lifeboat services for the years 1939-46 and *Lifeboat Gallantry, RNLI Medals and how they were won*, edited by Barry Cox and published by Spink at London in 1998.

Finally, I would like to thank Colin Mulvanna of the Maritime and Coastguard Agency and his team at the Langdon Battery as well as tug master John Reynolds for helping me with a great deal of background information and illustrations to support that material.

Those mentioned above, and many others that I have met with a seafaring background, have made this work a very interesting undertaking, helping to bring to life the dramas of wreck and rescue of many years ago and recalling vividly those of more recent times. Two wrecks remain paramount in the memories of the elder generation; the *Helena Modjeska* for the bounty of food that it yielded at a time of severe rationing, and the South Goodwin lightvessel No.90, the loss of whose seven-man crew touched many people both locally and further afield.

Introduction

This book explores and illustrates a notable selection of the many shipwrecks that have occurred in the Narrow Seas off the south-east coast of England and the closer shores of the continent. It follows an earlier work entitled *Shipwrecks of Kent*, which concentrated on the coastline and the sandbanks immediately offshore from that county, notably the Goodwin Sands.

Calamity Corner extends the coverage to the whole of the Thames Estuary as far north as Harwich and then reaches out to include the Belgian port of Zeebrugge, which has many connections with England, both glorious and tragic. After that port the Belgian and French coasts are followed south-westwards, remembering the events at Dunkirk in 1940, to terminate at Boulogne from where the commentary crosses to Beachy Head and finally covers further incidents on the English shores of East Sussex and Kent.

Innumerable maritime accidents have occurred in the waters of this region during war and peace. Any attempt to cover even a tenth of those known would result in a work which would become repetitive, as well as far beyond the scope of a volume of this size, even though the excitement and conditions of each wreck might not be exactly the same. The examples included here are the most infamous wrecks, or those that demonstrate most the courage displayed by people who sought to rescue those in distress. Inevitably, for completeness and because of their notoriety, a few of the casualties described in *Shipwrecks of Kent* are also included here, but in those cases different, and sometimes more dramatic, illustrations have been used.

The title of this book derives from a description given by the press to the southern section of the Goodwin Sands in the period after the Second World War when a series of wrecks of freighters occurred in a relatively short time. It is fair to extend this description to the larger area described above, as much shipping is concentrated into these narrow channels lined by sandbanks. The region resembles closely a distorted egg timer, where the constriction through which the sand must pass is called the Straits of Dover. Thus there has been and remains very little room for error, for, although the area is now almost all under continuous radar surveillance by coastguards and port control officers, major accidents still occur, as exemplified by the relatively recent sinking of the car carrier *Tricolor* as a result of a collision.

Over the period of three centuries covered by this work, the type of loss has changed from predominantly stranding on shore or sandbank to collisions, which often involved the sinking of one of the vessels involved. Two wooden sailing vessels could often survive such contact, but once iron hulls and steam power arrived the results of collision were much more serious.

The two world wars led to a great number of wrecks, both of naval and merchant ships. Passage of the Dover Straits by the German Navy was contested strongly between 1914 and 1918 and again between 1939 and 1945, leading to surface battles with the Dover patrol and the sinking of numerous U-boats by the Channel mine barrage in the earlier conflict.

Other major causes of casualties were the German mining campaign, the retreat from Dunkirk and the attacks on coastal convoys, which caused many losses among merchant ships during the early part of the Second World War. The impression gained is that almost the whole of the seabed in the line of the shipping channels must be covered with the remains of wrecks.

Inevitably, when dealing with an area where shipping is so abundant and accidents numerous, there have been some unusual events. Two Brocklebank Line steamers with the name *Mahratta*, on practically the same voyage, were wrecked on the Goodwin Sands thirty years apart. In 1909, the same year as the stranding of the first *Mahratta*, the cruiser HMS *Sappho* was in collision with the SS *Sappho* of the Ellerman Wilson Line off Dungeness, the naval vessel only surviving due t o great efforts by the Dover tugs. Finally, in that same period, the German five-mast sailing ship *Preussen*, then the largest sailing ship in the world, was wrecked at the South Foreland after a collision with the railway steamer *Brighton* and bad weather had left her uncontrollable.

Blockships are a peculiar category of wartime wreck because they are deliberate and were used in a number of ports, notably Zeebrugge and Dover. The SS *Spanish Prince* remains sunk near the western entrance of Dover Harbour to this day, but, interestingly, one intended blockship never fulfilled its role. The ageing Canadian Pacific liner *Montrose*, which had earlier conveyed Dr Crippen and his lady friend to Canada, was intended for such use in 1914. However, before it could be sunk in the harbour entrance, it broke away from the Prince of Wales Pier in a gale, drifted through all the moored naval craft without touching anything, then out through the eastern entrance to become another wreck on the Goodwin Sands.

In order to simplify the various casualties, *Calamity Corner* is divided into different categories of accident. These are rather arbitrary because some ships were unlucky enough to suffer more than one type of misfortune at the time of the accident. In the case of some collisions involving tankers, for instance, fire followed immediately. On other occasions a victim of a collision may have been put ashore to prevent it from sinking.

It is important firstly to examine some of the most serious incidents that have happened together with the causes:

Major maritime disasters that have occurred off south-east England and the near coast of Europe:

Name	Type of ship	Date	Place	Lives lost*	Cause
Bulwark	Battleship	11/1914	River Medway	729	Explosion
Princess Alice	Paddle steamer	9/1878	River Thames	640	Collision
Vryheid (Du.)	Troopship	11/1802	Dymchurch	454	Stranding
Restoration	Third-rate warship	11/1703	Goodwin Sands	386	Storm
Princess Irene	Minelayer	5/1915	River Medway	c.350	Explosion
Aurora	Troopship	12/1805	Goodwin Sands	300+	Stranding
Northfleet	Emigrant ship	1/1873	Off Dymchurch	320	Collision
Emile Deschamps (Fr.)	Minesweeper	6/1940	Off Margate	300+	Mine
Grösser Kürfürst (Ge.)	Ironclad warship	5/1878	Off Folkestone	284	Collision
Stirling Castle	Third-rate warship	11/1703	Goodwin Sands	279	Storm
Mary	Fourth-rate warship	11/1703	Goodwin Sands	272	Storm
Northumberland	Third-rate warship	11/1703	Goodwin Sands	253	Storm
Floridian (Am.)	Emigrant ship	2/1849	Long Sand	193	Stranding
Herald of Free Enterprise	Cross-Channel Ferry	3/1987	Zeebrugge	188	Capsize
Maloja	Passenger vessel	2/1916	Off Dover	155	Mine
Pavon (Fr.)	Cargo vessel	5/1940	Near Calais	152	Air attack
Anglia	Hospital ship	11/1915	Off Folkestone	134	Mine
W.A. Scholten (Ge.)	Passenger vessel	11/1887	Off Dover	132	Collision
Carlisle	Fourth-rate warship	9/1700	The Downs	124	Explosion
Simon Bolivar (Du.)	Passenger vessel	11/1939	Off Harwich	84	Mine
Glatton	Monitor	9/1918	Dover	77	Explosion
Deutschland (Ge.)	Passenger vessel	12/1875	Long Sand	57	Stranding

Moldavia	Auxiliary cruiser	5/1918	Off Beachy	56	Torpedo Head
Pommerania (Ge.)	Passenger vessel	11/1878	Off Dover	48	Collision

*Note: The number of lives reported lost from these casualties tends to vary according to the source that is consulted, so these figures cannot be taken as absolute. Where available, the figures quoted are taken from Hocking's *Dictionary of Disasters at Sea*.

Warship Casualties

While this section covers mostly actions and incidents that have occurred in wartime, there have also been major naval losses in peacetime. Given the relatively short periods of war and the long periods of peace this is perhaps understandable. The most significant incident overall was the loss of the four ships of Admiral Beaumont's fleet wrecked on the Goodwins in the great storm of 1703 at a cost of some 1,200 lives. Another tragic incident was the sinking of the German battleship *Grösser Kürfurst* by collision off Folkestone on her maiden voyage. The 1909 collision involving HMS *Sappho* has already been mentioned, but, additionally, the destroyer HMS *Blackwater* sank off Dungeness in April of the same year after being struck by SS *Hero*.

Even during hostilities ships have been lost due to a great variety of causes. Explosions have taken their toll, the most infamous being the loss of HMS *Bulwark* in the river Medway in 1914, as it involved the highest loss of life of any single wreck in this region, roughly half the toll of the *Titanic*. HM *Torpedo Boat No.4* was lost with fourteen of her crew at Ramsgate on 26 May 1917 due to a torpedo explosion. The monitor HMS *Glatton* capsized in Dover Harbour following a mysterious explosion in September 1918, again with the loss of a large number of lives.

Mines have taken their fair share of victims as well, HMS *Blanche* being the first destroyer loss of the Second World War when she sank off Margate. Not long afterwards the minesweeper HMS *Mastiff* was lost while trying to retrieve a magnetic mine for examination.

Many British, French and German warships were lost in the Straits of Dover during the two world wars, the worst period for the French and British Navies during the last conflict being the withdrawal from Dunkirk.

In the end, some older warships were subordinated to the roll of blockships, and in this form were sunk to seal the port of Zeebrugge during the assault of St George's Day 1918. The cruiser HMS *Vindictive* was reduced to a floating wreck in this battle, but was sailed back and then used again as a blockship at Ostend, contributing greatly to the most glorious moment for the Navy in these waters since the time of the Spanish Armada.

Mercantile Victims of War

Inevitably, the local cost of two world wars in losses by the mercantile marine of many nations was very high. Shipwrecks occurred both due to enemy action, primarily in the laying of mines, but also due to accidental collisions and groundings in congested areas where many of the major lights had been extinguished.

While significant losses of major vessels were fewer in the First World War, one of the most notorious sinkings was that of the hospital ship *Anglia*, mined between Dover and Folkestone, apparently only a few days after it had brought King George V back from France with a minor injury. Another significant loss was that of the P&O liner *Moldavia*, converted to an armed merchant cruiser and sunk by UB-57 in May 1918.

Mines claimed four intermediate passenger liners in the approaches to the Thames in the early months of the Second World War. Casualties were numerous aboard the Dutch *Simon Bolivar*, but passengers aboard the Holland-America Line's *Spaarndam* fared better. The Japanese *Terukuni Maru* sank off Harwich and the *Dunbar Castle* off Broadstairs also with relatively few casualties, although those aboard the latter were serious.

Although much has been reported of British losses of ships large and small at Dunkirk, many French ships were lost also, notably the SS *Pavon* of Société Orbigny which was bombed and beached near Calais while carrying many injured French and Dutch troops. The vessel was burnt out and it is believed that no absolute figure for those killed was ever established. Another victim of the evacuation was the minesweeper *Emile Deschamps*, sunk by mines while approaching Margate packed with evacuees. Again the loss of life was considerable and the total uncertain owing to no one having made an initial count of those aboard.

It is no exaggeration to suggest that at least one hundred ships must have been sunk by mines in this latter conflict. Later aircraft attacks were to take their toll of Channel convoys until August 1940 when passages of ships through the eastern Channel ceased until after the D-Day invasion. Losses then resumed, a number of Liberty ships becoming victims.

A Saga of Collisions

Collisions between ships have always occurred, but the severity of such events grew greater as their speed and size increased. Until the nineteenth century most losses were due to ships being driven ashore due to stress of weather or poor navigation. However, during the later Victorian years and Edwardian period there were frequent disastrous collisions involving steam ships. There were also steamers in collision with sailing ships that led to the sinking of the former with a significant loss of life. This is not entirely surprising as large sailing ships often also had iron hulls.

Both the German Hamburg-America liner *Pommerania* (1878) and the Holland-America emigrant ship *W.A. Scholten* (1887) sank off Dover after collisions with sailing vessels. Later the P&O steamer *Oceana* went down off Eastbourne after colliding with the German Laitz barque *Pisagua* off Beachy Head. However, in the latter case the sailing vessel was lucky to survive, having incurred greater damage to her bow than that incurred by the less fortunate five-mast *Preussen* of the same fleet a few years earlier. Excluding the periods of hostilities, serious collisions occurred at the rate of at least twenty a year during the years that followed. Finally, it was the dramatic collision between the Peruvian freighter *Paracas* and the tanker *Texaco Caribbean* in 1971, with the loss of two further ships that hit the sunken wreckage of the latter vessel, which led to the introduction of a mandatory Channel separation scheme. Continuous surveillance of the Straits by the coastguards also commenced at that time.

In spite of this action, collisions remain the chief cause of marine casualties in the Thames Estuary and Dover Straits. Recent serious incidents have involved the ferry *European Gateway* off Harwich, the *British Trent* off the Scheldt, the *Norwegian Dream* off Zeebrugge and most recently the *Tricolor-Kariba* incident off Dunkirk. In this last case two other ships later struck the buoyed wreck, the *Nicola* and the oil tanker *Vicky*, in a scenario vividly reminiscent of the *Texaco Caribbean*, although fortunately there was no loss of life in this recent disaster. The recovery of the sunken *Tricolor* by Smit-Tak is proving to be one of the most demanding salvage projects of all time.

Nowadays, there is a tendency for ships to pass through the Straits in groups on very similar courses. Such clumping can often produce close quarter situations which may result in bow-stern collisions. Strangely, electronic aids like global positioning systems appear at times to increase the risk of collision rather than reduce it, as they give different vessels identical courses between waypoints. This concern is not exactly new, for a similar criticism was at one time levelled at the Decca Navigator.

Ships Ashore

Ships have been driven ashore by gales, or put on a beach or sandbank to prevent them from sinking, throughout the time that men have sailed the seas. More often than not those wrecks have been completely demolished, sometimes the timbers being put to other purposes. In contrast, ironically, it is occasionally due to these events that interesting ancient craft have been preserved, at least in part.

The area described in this work is particularly rich in historic wrecks. The Bronze Age boat at Dover may well have been put ashore at the end of a useful life, before her much later discovery under the buildings of what is now Townwall Street. Evidence of a cargo of similar age has been found in Langdon Bay just to the east of Dover Harbour. Unfortunately, in this case the wooden vessel carrying it has completely rotted away.

Were it not for the great storm wreck of the man-of-war *Stirling Castle* in November 1703 the numerous artefacts raised from that vessel would not have been available.

Numerous East Indiamen have been driven ashore along the south-east coast, ranging from the *Hindostan* and *Active* (1803), *Walpole* (1808) and *Albion* off the Isle of Thanet to the *Admiral Gardner* and *Britannia* (1809) on the Goodwin Sands and the Dutch *Amsterdam* (1749) at Bulverhythe near Hastings. These wrecks have also yielded many items of considerable interest, ranging from spoons to guns and personal items such as clothes and shoes.

In addition to these major wrecks, there have been constant and frequent casualties among smaller vessels throughout the ages. Sometimes their crews were lucky, if stranded on an offshore bank, to be picked up by a passing ship before their craft broke up, otherwise they were lost without trace. If they drove ashore in really bad weather, when there was a huge surf pounding on the beach, they could often drown in sight of the crowds that wished to save them, as happened with the tragic case of the *Vryheid*. It was to help those facing such dire situations that the National Lifeboat Institution was founded in 1824. The specially constructed boats that were introduced as a result saved many lives on the south-east coast from that time onwards.

Coming nearer to the present day, disabled vessels were put ashore along the coast, particularly at Deal, after being disabled by bombs and mines during the war.

During the first half of the twentieth century the main area of stranding remained the infamous Goodwin Sands, which still claimed the occasional victim until as late as 1975. Nowadays it is rare for ships to be driven ashore on either of the English or French coasts but these events do still occur, as exemplified by the Dover-Calais ferry *Stena Challenger*, which ran aground just outside the port of Calais in 1997.

Fires Aboard Ship

Shipboard fires are particularly feared by mariners as they can easily render a ship uninhabitable or lead to it sinking. They arise primarily from four main causes: spontaneous ignition of the cargo, electrical faults, catastrophic engine failure and collision with another ship. There are also the possibilities of carelessness among passengers and crew and arson but these cases are generally far fewer.

Two ferries have been casualties of fire in this region: the *Onward*, which capsized in Folkestone Harbour in September 1918, and the Danish *Kronprins Frederick* which was engulfed while alongside Parkeston Quay at Harwich in April 1953. Two hundred firemen from all over Essex fought the latter fire, which also led to the capsize of the ship. Despite the damage, both vessels were raised and rebuilt for further service.

During the first half of the twentieth century, fires were fairly frequent in peacetime and it was such an occurrence that led to the loss of the general steam vessel *Falcon* on the shore at Langdon Bay, Dover. A fire in her cargo of hemp and matches became a conflagration which blazed from stem to stern. The *Yousuf Baksh* was another vessel to suffer a fire in her hemp cargo, which reduced her to a smouldering wreck. Around 1962 the Turkish *Kayseri* was brought into Dover with her linseed cargo afire. It took eight 8in pumps to control the outbreak but the ship was saved from total loss on that occasion.

In recent years, the most serious fires have been caused by collisions. In June 1993, the laden tanker *British Trent* was swept by fire after a collision off Ostend, resulting in the loss of nine lives. When the cruise ship *Norwegian Dream* struck the container ship *Ever Decent* not so far from the same position, a serious fire was caused aboard the *Ever Decent* which burned for almost a week. Although there were no casualties on this occasion, the extremely varied contents of the containers caused problems in fighting the fire. The materials encountered included motor tyres, gin and cyanide and these needed careful consideration in terms of the health hazard from the copious amount of smoke that was generated.

The Rescuers, the Price and the Prizes

Over the timescale of this book the saving of lives at sea has gradually progressed from at best a perfunctory exercise, when the salvage of a valuable cargo might take precedence, to the highly refined service that exists today.

Every sea-girt region of the British Isles has its tales of heroism in the act of lifesaving from shipwrecks and the south-east coast of England and the closer coasts of Europe have probably more than most. In fact, the combination of low flat areas of coastline with high, steep cliffs where no beach exists has led to a versatile group of lifesavers, whether they be fishermen, coastguards or lifeboatmen.

The lifeboat was invented by Lionel Lukin in 1785. After that date a number of ports and coastal resorts purchased boats designed by Henry Greathead. The formation of the National Lifeboat Service in 1824 led to the further introduction of specially designed boats adapted to work in rough water close to shore or sandbanks, which offered a lower risk than the luggers and other sailing craft had faced in previously carrying out this work. They were, however, often crewed by the same men as fished in those boats or put pilots aboard ships on a normal working day. As the nineteenth century progressed, brave incidents of lifesaving became more common and received widespread publicity in the press. The presentation of medals to men who were successful in saving crews from wrecks on sandbanks under the worst storm conditions imaginable lent some prestige and also glamour to these acts.

Lifeboats appeared on the Kent, Sussex and Essex coasts from around 1800 onwards, the greatest number being in place over the period 1850-1925. Initially some were private ventures, but gradually all were taken over by the RNLI. Over the years they have achieved glory and suffered tragedy. In 1881 the Ramsgate lifeboat *Bradford* was successful in saving the remaining crew of the ship *Indian Chief*, wrecked on the Long Sand in atrocious weather. The complete crew of tug and lifeboat received silver medals and coxswain Charles Fish a gold medal. This service was one of the most notable ever carried out by a British lifeboat. In sharp contrast, the Rye Harbour boat *Mary Stanford*, after launching in November 1928 to a ship which was soon found to have got out of difficulties, capsized on her return to harbour, drowning all seventeen aboard, twelve of whom were aged less than thirty years.

Aside from these brief moments of triumph and tragedy, the lifeboatmen, fishermen, crews of tugs, pilot boats and other craft have over the years rescued thousands of people in distress in fairly routine events which have not achieved great public acclaim. Wartime also brought its own particular demands, which included the Margate and Ramsgate lifeboats being taken to Dunkirk by their own coxswains and others by naval personnel.

Nowadays, fatalities amongst the crews of commercial ships are rare and it is those who seek pleasure in sailing, diving or other water sports who are most at risk.

In conclusion, it is clearly impossible to even mention all the brave acts that have occurred in these Narrow Seas in war and peace, so numerous have they been. The simple epitaph written for Charles Troughton, who drowned in the Margate surf-lifeboat disaster of November 1897, ends this introduction:

Greater love hath no man than this: that a man lay down his life for his friends.

Applied singly then, it has also applied to many others before and since.

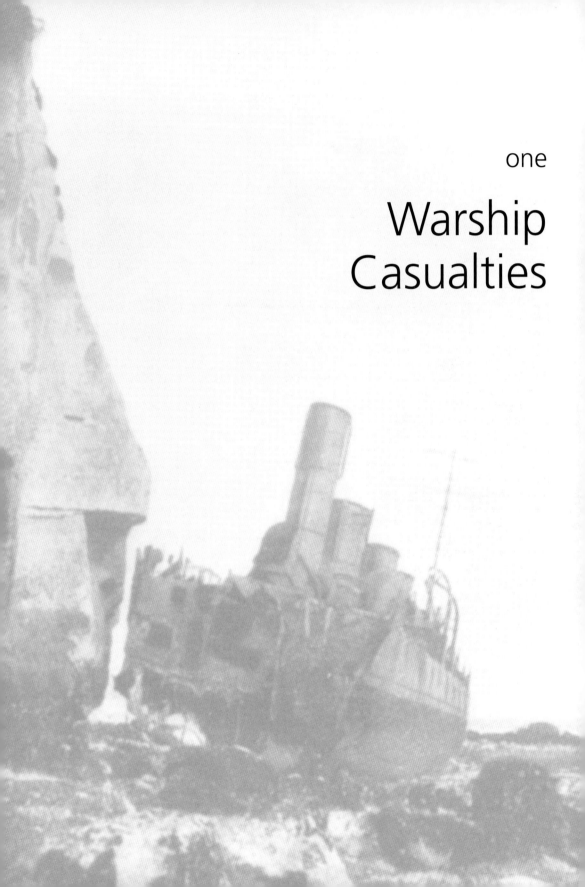

one

Warship
Casualties

There have been few battles in British waters in which this country has not been involved, but one instance was the action in the Downs between the Dutch and the Spanish in 1639. Creeping up under cover of fog, Admiral Tromp inflicted severe damage on the Spanish fleet, several ships being sunk, others taken as prizes, and about twenty driven ashore around Deal. (C.J. Visscher)

It was during an Anglo-Dutch skirmish with the French in 1690 that the third-rate warship *Anne* of seventy guns suffered severe damage. In order to prevent her being taken as a prize or burnt by French fire ships she was set afire by her commander Captain John Tyrell. Her remains can still be seen on the shore off Pett Level near Hastings. The above illustration is taken from a recent painting by Richard Endsor. (Shipwreck Heritage Museum, Hastings)

The most costly series of wrecks in terms of human life to occur in this region were the losses of the seventy-gun third-rate warships *Stirling Castle, Restoration, Northumberland* and fourth-rate *Mary* with Admiral Beaumont on the Goodwin Sands during the great storm of November 1703. Some 1,200 men were lost in total, only about eighty being saved and these coming mostly from the *Stirling Castle*. This unusual contemporary painting appears to show survivors trying to reach the exposed Goodwin Sands, a very uncertain place of refuge which offered only a slim chance of rescue. (National Maritime Museum)

The anchored brig *Dorothy* was deliberately destroyed on 15 October 1805 off Walmer Castle in a demonstration by the American Robert Fulton of his invention of a submarine bomb or torpedo. The result was achieved with a floating bomb containing 180lbs of gunpowder. As the Battle of Trafalgar occurred only a few days later, the British Navy continued to rely on conventional warfare for some time afterwards.

The German central citadel warship *Grösser Kurfürst* had been completed on 6 May 1878 and was sunk by collision off Folkestone just twenty-five days later on 31 May. Hence there are very few pictures of her and that shown above is of her sister *Friedrich der Grosse*. These were the days when steam power was combined with sail, but the ship was using only her engines at the time.

The *König Wilhelm* was a larger vessel, being the flagship of Rear-Admiral von Batsch, commanding officer of the squadron commissioned for service in Turkish waters. She escaped with her bowsprit smashed and her ram bow badly twisted. Being holed, she took in a great deal of water forward but was able to reach Portsmouth where she went into dry dock.

Opposite below: The iron-clad *Grösser Kurfürst* was sailing in close company with the other German warships *König Wilhelm* and *Preussen* off Folkestone, when they were approached by two sailing vessels. In the resulting avoidance manoeuvres the *König Wilhelm* struck the *Grösser Kurfürst* on the port side amidships with her ram bow, the damage being such that the latter sank within eight minutes. Despite numerous craft being in the vicinity, 284 officers and men out of a total crew of 497 were lost.

Right: Those who died in the sinking of the *Grösser Kurfürst* were interred in this communal grave in Folkestone cemetery. On his return to Germany, Rear-Admiral von Batsch was court-martialled and sentenced to six months' imprisonment for culpable neglect but was pardoned after serving only fourteen days. (A.L.)

Another naval vessel to suffer a serious collision was the cruiser HMS *Sappho* (3,400 tons), struck by a merchant ship of the same name in fog off Dungeness on 19 June 1909. Left in a sinking condition, she was kept afloat by the pumps of the Dover tugs *Lady Crundall* and *Herculaneum* and was successfully brought into that harbour; most of her crew being previously brought ashore by the Dungeness lifeboats. (J.C. Craik)

The SS *Sappho* (1,694 grt) was owned by the Ellerman Wilson Line. It was a most peculiar coincidence that this vessel, which was on a voyage from Hull to the Mediterranean, should strike a warship of the same name. Ironically, she suffered little damage and continued on her voyage. Only two months earlier the destroyer HMS *Blackwater* had been sunk in a similar collision but on that occasion the colliding vessel was the SS *Hero*, an unfortunate name. (World Ship Society)

A further victim of collision was the French submarine *Pluviose*, which surfaced just ahead of the cross-Channel steamer *Pas de Calais*, bound for Dover on 26 May 1910. After being struck off her home port, the bow of the Calais-based *Pluviose* rose up at an angle of 45° and disappeared after about ten minutes taking all twenty-seven crew down with her. This smaller submarine of 398 tons had been launched from the Arsenal de Cherbourg in May 1907. She was subsequently raised and returned to service until disposal in 1919. There were some thirty-four submarines in her class, of which a representative picture is shown here. (Janes Fighting Ships)

The impressive monument in Calais dedicated 'Aux Marins du *Pluviose* Morts pour la Patrie'. Those lost were: Capitaine de Frégate Prat; Lieutenant de Vaisseau Callot; Enseigne de Vaisseau Engel; Premiers Maîtres Fontaine et Le Prunennec; Maîtres Mécaniciens Gras et Moren; Seconds Maîtres Appéré, Bresillon, Chandat, Delpierre, Gauchet, Henry, Huet, Le Breton, Le Floch, C.; Le Floch, P.; Le Moal, Le Moine, Liot, Manach, Moulin, Scollan et Warin; Quartier Maîtres Batard et Gautier; Matelot Cuisinier Carbon. (A.L.)

HMS *Niger* is the first casualty of war described in these pages. She was apparently torpedoed by Kapitanleutnant Walther Forstmann, a First World War U-boat ace, aboard U-12. The *Niger* was engaged in boarding duties for contraband control purposes in the Downs and, as she was anchored for a good deal of the time, offered a tempting target. The Deal galley punt *Hope*, normally licensed for ten passengers, took forty-four survivors off the *Niger* and managed to keep afloat in the rough sea until her crew could transfer them to other craft.

The Secretary of the Admiralty made the following announcement on 11 November 1914:

> *HMS* Niger *(Lieutenant-Commander Arthur P. Muir, RN) was torpedoed by a submarine this morning in the Downs and foundered.*
> *All the officers and seventy-seven of the crew were saved. Two men are severely and two slightly injured.*
> *It is thought there was no loss of life.*
> *HMS* Niger *was a torpedo-gunboat of 810 tons, built in 1892. She was employed in semi-combatant duties.*

The *Niger* was lying about two miles out from Deal when torpedoed by a German submarine, in a direct line with the long pier, where crowds had assembled at the sound of heavy fire. In all about 100 boats set out immediately for the ship, which was enveloped by a dense mist of black smoke, and though there was a high wind and the work of rescue was dangerous, British pluck won through, and shortly after the disaster only eight were missing. The men, it seems, were having a meal on the *Niger* when violent shaking occurred, and before it was actually known that the boat had been torpedoed the crew were in the lifeboats by the captain's orders. The *Niger* had been at anchor there for some time. She did not sink rapidly, and it was fully half an hour before she reluctantly went under.

In contrast to the sinking of the *Niger* where casualties were few, the catastrophic explosion which destroyed the 15,000-ton battleship *Bulwark* in the river Medway caused the highest loss of life of any single ship incident in these Narrow Seas. Two of the fourteen rescued later died. Her wreck lies close to the head of Bee Ness jetty in Kethole Reach, not far from the remains in Saltpan Reach of the *Princess Irene*, the explosion of which claimed almost 400 lives in 1915.

The tragic loss of the *Bulwark* on 26 November 1914 was announced in the House of Commons by Mr Churchill the same day in the following terms:

> *I regret to say I have some bad news for the House. The* Bulwark *battleship, which was lying at Sheerness this morning, blew up at 7.53 a.m. The Vice and Rear Admirals, who were present, have reported their conviction that it was an internal magazine explosion which rent the ship asunder. There was apparently no upheaval in the water, and the ship had entirely disappeared when the smoke had cleared away. An inquiry will be held tomorrow which may possibly throw more light on the occurrence.*
>
> *The loss of the ship does not sensibly affect the military position, but I regret to say the loss of life is very severe. Only twelve men are saved. All the officers and the rest of the crew, who I suppose amounted to between 700 and 800, have perished.*
>
> *I think the House would wish me to express on their behalf the deep sympathy and sorrow with which the House has heard the news, and the sympathy they feel with those who have lost their relatives and friends.*

In violence and horror the explosion was unprecedented. The band of the *Excellent* Gunnery School was playing for breakfast and some men were drilling on deck when it occurred. A great sheet of flame and quantities of debris shot upwards, and when the smoke cleared away the battleship had disappeared from the sea, leaving only wreckage flung far and wide. Fourteen NCOs and men were saved. About thirty bodies were recovered from the Medway the next day. The *Bulwark* (captain Guy Slater) was a representative ship of the older pre-Dreadnought type. Laid down at Devonport in March 1899 and launched in the following October, she was completed for service in 1902. She cost slightly over £1 million.

The destroyers of the Dover Patrol faced hazard every day in the Straits and skirmishes with similar German vessels were fairly frequent once Zeebrugge had been occupied. On the night of 26 October 1916 there was a full-scale assault in which HMS *Flirt* was sunk and the Tribal Class HMS *Nubian*, shown above, had her bows blown off by a torpedo. This latter vessel was taken in tow but broke away in the bad weather and drove ashore near St Margaret's Bay. The after part was refloated but the remains of the forepart were left under the cliffs.

Fifteen of the crew of HMS *Nubian* were either killed or missing. One of these, William Smith, died as a result of wounds received in the battle of 26 October. He is buried in St James's Cemetery, Dover. There were only nine survivors from the sixty-seven men aboard HMS *Flirt*. (A.L.)

Above: A section of her bow plating provides a different kind of memorial to HMS *Nubian*. It still lies under the cliffs between St Margaret's Bay and South Foreland. (A.L.)

Right: Those also missing from HMS *Nubian* were: James Bushell, W. Broomfield, J. Davies, L. Horsley, W. Keeling, F.H.J. Knight, W. Minors, L.E. Pronger, J. Rapson, F. Sayers, J. Sharp. J.W. Smith, W.G. Wavell and Stoker Alfred James Clewley who is also buried in St James's Cemetery at Dover. (A.L.)

Other remains of HMS *Nubian* which lie beneath the cliffs include what appears to be the steam cylinder from the forward Thornycroft water-tube boiler of the destroyer. Built in 1909, and displacing 1,062 ton, the vessel developed 15,500 HP to give a maximum speed of thirty-four knots. (A.L.)

A typical water-tube boiler of the period showing the position of the steam cylinder, at upper centre, and the boiler tubes at left.

Now broken and twisted between the fallen chalk blocks, the boiler tubes of HMS *Nubian* are still recognizable in the place they have lain for nearly ninety years. It took the efforts of a large team of Royal Engineers with explosives to clear a way for the stern of the ship to be refloated all those years ago. (A.L.)

The recovered stern of HMS *Nubian* was joined at Chatham Dockyard in 1917 to the bow of sister vessel HMS *Zulu* which had lost hers from contact with a mine. The combination was renamed *Zubian*, which went on to serve for the rest of the war but was disposed of shortly afterwards.

Another victim of the clash of 26 October 1916 was the drifter *Roburn*. Frank Brown from Caister was aged eighteen at the time and became one of the youngest naval prisoners of war. This account is taken from his unpublished autobiography. Other drifters lost during this battle were: *Spotless Prince, Ajax II, Gleaner of the Sea, Launch Out* and *Datum*.

The sinking of the drifter *Roburn*, one of the smaller craft of the Dover Patrol, on the night of 26 October 1916 – A personal account by Frank Brown.

I remember the night of the escape of the German destroyers from Zeebrugge and how the Roburn *became involved in that disaster to some of the drifters; I believe the auxiliary ship* The Queen *was also destroyed.*

There were ten members of the crew, eight from Caister and two from Yarmouth. Ben Haylett was skipper, Virgin Brown was mate (he was a distant cousin of my father). Ernest Haylett, brother of Ben, was Chief Engineer; Alfred Cook was second engineer and Elijah Saunders was boatswain. There was also Charles Simmons, Stanley Youngs, Mr Nutson and Mr Clover/Glover (both from Yarmouth) and myself as cook.

I think it was the second night of our patrol, about 12 p.m., as I was asleep down in the cabin (as cabin boy I did not take watches), when one of the crew shouted to get up for the Germans were upon us. This is a most extraordinary thing, for as a sound sleeper I never heard a thing as a young lad.

It was a chilly night on that 26 October, with the wind freshening, yet twice I had been on deck to the surprise of Ben Haylett who was on watch. I think he was disturbed that more than once he had to order me down to the cabin, because it was so unusual to see me after I'd once turned in. Just before midnight I heard gunfire and then the sudden call of the second engineer, Alfred Cook, for all hands on deck. I quickly got out of the bunk, pulled on my trousers and went on deck. It is certain that was the only call made and had I been sound asleep as I usually was then I cannot imagine escaping with my life. As I came out of the cabin the engine room was full of escaping steam, and the ship's gunwales were almost level with the water, but she was steady, not on her side, and sinking without any apparent list whatsoever.

Virgin Brown said, 'Run forward and get a lifebelt,' for all the belts were hung in front of the wheelhouse, and it was when my arm was up to pull it from the line that a piece of shrapnel must have hit me in the face, breaking my nose and really putting me out, or at least leaving me semi-conscious, but Mr Brown picked me up and hurried me aft and with the help of Mr Saunders laid me at the bottom of a small boat, where I remained until the German destroyer picked us up. I shall always remember that Virgin Brown was the coolest member of the crew – he seemed to be completely in control in directing operations while Ben Haylett got into the boat, obviously to take it away from the ship. I never knew whether or not all the crew got into the boat until long afterwards. The men pulled away from the ship, but how long we were pulling for I have no idea. I was conscious of little of what went on after I was wounded.

The next thing I knew I was on board a German destroyer, in their operating theatre with the surgeon of the ship examining my face. He tried to stop the flow of blood, because I found it hard to breathe, having to breathe through my mouth until I was actually in hospital, quite ill, in Bruges.

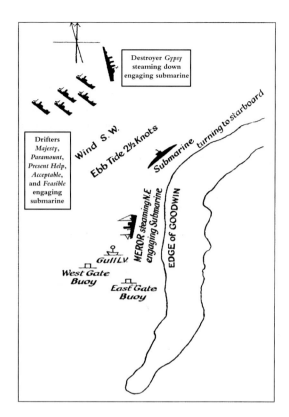

The Ramsgate drifters were able to even the score in November 1917 by bravely attacking the 725-ton German submarine U–48 which had had the misfortune to ground on the Goodwin Sands and was trying to escape. After being repeatedly hit by shells from the six-pounder guns of the drifters and assisted by fire from the destroyer *Gipsy*, the survivors of the crew of the submarine abandoned ship and were captured. Although the U–48 had the superior armament, it was unable to make effective use of it, considering that six lesser-armed ships were attacking it. (*The Auxiliary Patrol*, E. Keble Chatterton)

A drifter (foreground) and two trawlers of the Dover Patrol moored in Dover Harbour during the First World War. These wooden fishing vessels averaged only 80-90 grt and were very lightly armed but, as they guarded the cross-Channel mined net-barrage, they were occasionally involved in close-quarter battles of great ferocity. The Admiralty awarded £1,000 to each of the crews of the vessels involved in the sinking of U–48. Three of the drifter skippers received the DSC as well.

When the U-48 was scuttled, only twenty-two of the forty-three aboard were rescued. Her commander, Captain-Lieutenant Carl Edeling, chose not to be one of them. As was the fate of many other ships, the submarine remained on the Goodwin Sands and was largely forgotten; then, unexpectedly in 1973, she re-emerged to public view. Within a year or so the sands had claimed her again. (Chris Fright)

As a consequence of the increasingly effective Channel mine-barrage between Folkestone and Cap Gris Nez, many German submarines were destroyed in the Straits of Dover and southern North Sea. This illustration of a survivor, UB-21, serves as an example of the smaller submarines of 263 tons. She is shown at Ramsgate on 16 December 1918 after her surrender.

German submarine losses during the First World War in the Southern North Sea and Eastern English Channel:

U-Boat	Position of loss	Date	Cause
U-11	Dover Straits	9/12/1914	Mined
U-5	Eastern English Channel	18/12/1914	Mined
U-8	Dover Straits	4/3/1915	Sunk by destroyers *Maori* and *Gurkha*
UC-9	Southern North Sea	21/10/1915	Mined
UC-61	Stranded near Cap Gris Nez	11/11/1916	Scuttled
UC-19	Dover Straits	6/12/1916	Sunk by destroyer HMS *Llewellyn*
UC-46	Dover Straits	8/2/1917	Sunk by destroyer HMS *Liberty*
UC-26	Thames Estuary	9/5/1917	Sunk by destroyers *Milne*, *Mentor* and *Miranda*
UC-36	Off Hinder lightvessel	20/5/1917	Bombed by seaplanes
UB-57	Off Zeebrugge	21/6/1917	Mined
UC-1	Thames Estuary off Sunk lightvessel	25/7/1917	Bombed by seaplanes
UC-72	Thames Estuary off Sunk lightvessel	22/9/1917	Bombed by seaplanes
UC-21	Off North Foreland	27/9/1917	Sunk in mined nets
UC-6	Thames Estuary off Sunk lightvessel	28/9/1917	Bombed by seaplanes
UC-14	Off Zeebrugge	3/10/1917	Mined
UC-65	Dover Straits	3/11/1917	Torpedoed by submarine HMS C-15
U-48	Goodwin Sands	24/11/1917	Sank after attack by drifters of Dover Patrol and destroyer HMS *Gipsy*
UB-56	Dover Straits	19/12/1917	Sunk in minefield
U-109	Dover Straits	26/1/1918	Gunfire of drifter *Beryl III* and mines
UB-35	Dover Straits	26/1/1918	Depth charges from destroyer HMS *Leven*
UC-50	Off Dungeness	4/2/1918	Sunk by destroyer HMS *Zubian*
UB-38	Dover Straits	8/2/1918	Mined in barrage
UB-58	Dover Straits	10/3/1918	Mined in barrage
UB-33	Dover Straits	11/4/1918	Mined in barrage
UB-55	Dover Straits	22/4/1918	Mined in barrage
UC-79	Dover Straits	22/4/1918	Mined in barrage
UB-31	Dover Straits	2/5/1918	Sunk by depth charges of drifters: *Lord Leitrim*, *Loyal Friend* and *Ocean Roamer*
UC-78	Dover Straits	2/5/1918	Sunk by depth charges of drifters: *Mary*, *BTB* and *Our Friend*
UC-64	Dover Straits	20/6/1918	Mined in barrage
UC-77	Dover Straits	10/7/1918	Sunk by depth charges of drifters: *Kessingland*, *Golden Gain* and three others
UB-109	Dover Straits	29/8/1918	Mined in barrage
UB-103	Dover Straits	16/9/1918	Sunk by depth charges of drifters: *Young Crow*, *Calceolaria*, *East Holme*, *East Anglia*, *Pleasant* and *Fertility*

Note: In addition the submarines UB-10, UB-40, UB-59 and UC-4 were scuttled in the Belgian ports of Bruges, Ostende and Zeebrugge on the evacuation of the German forces.

Above: One of the most famous Naval exploits of the First World War was the storming of the mole at Zeebrugge on 23 April 1918 and the blocking of that port. The ship chosen by Admiral Keyes to carry the attacking force to the mole was the elderly light cruiser *Vindictive* of 5,750 tons. (Cribb)

Left: Commanding officer of the *Vindictive* was Captain A.F.B. Carpenter RN, who 'walked around the decks directing operations and encouraging the men in the most dangerous and exposed positions. By his encouragement to those under him, his power of command and personal bearing, he undoubtedly contributed greatly to the success of the operation'. These words form part of the official record in support of his award of the Victoria Cross.

Opposite above: After the successful attack on Zeebrugge the cruiser *Vindictive* was sailed back to Dover. She had sustained severe damage and still carried most of those killed aboard her. In total, 156 dead and 400 wounded were brought ashore. At one period the cruiser was being hit every few seconds, chiefly in the superstructure, where splinters caused many casualties. Her bridge was smashed beyond recognition and her funnels were riddled.

Right: Robert Rosoman was First Lieutenant of the *Vindictive* at Zeebrugge. He had been involved deeply in the preparation of the ship for the raid and was very concerned when the first attempt was called off. He was also worried that the ship was rising and falling about 4ft alongside the mole as the landing occurred, causing casualties before the men were ashore. Hit in both legs, he continued his duties as the ship withdrew after fifty-five minutes alongside, refusing to leave the conning tower until they were well clear, commenting, 'The medicos have many men to deal with who want help far more than I do.' (Bassano)

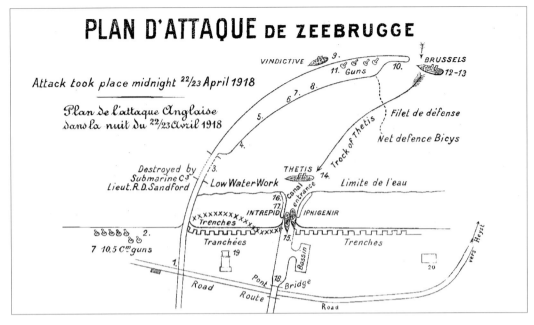

PLAN D'ATTAQUE DE ZEEBRUGGE

Attack took place midnight ²²/₂₃ April 1918

Plan de l'attaque Anglaise dans la nuit du ²²/₂₃ Avril 1918

VINDICTIVE 9.
11. Guns 10.
BRUSSELS 12-13
6. 7. 8.
5.
4.
Filet de défense
Net defence Bicys
Track of Thetis

Destroyed by 3.
Submarine C³
Lieut. R.D.Sandford
Low Water Work
THETIS 14.
Canal entrance
Limite de l'eau

16.
17.
INTREPID IPHIGENIR
xxxxxxx Trenches xxx
xxxx
xxxxx 15.
7 10.5 Cᵐguns 2.
Tranchées
19
Trenches
vers Heyst
20

1.
Road Route
Pont 18. Bridge
Bassin
Road

A general plan of the port of Zeebrugge showing the positions of the *Vindictive* and the various blockships after the attack. The numbers on the plan refer to others in this series of postcards from an album by J. Revyn of Brussels. Pictures from that album also appear on the opposite page.

Engineer Commander William Bury RN, who was appointed as Chief Engineer of the *Vindictive*, was also responsible for the preparation of the ship for the raid. Only he and Robert Rosoman were involved in the operation for a long period. Having been gassed briefly but otherwise escaping injury at Zeebrugge, he volunteered to sink the ship to block the harbour at Ostend, where he was seriously wounded by machine-gun fire while leaving her.

In spite of the cost in human life, the Zeebrugge raid was a brilliant success with nearly all the objectives achieved, most of which involved the sinking of blockships in strategically important places. One of these, the *Thetis*, a second-class cruiser of 3,400 tons built in 1890, was sunk at the entrance to the Brugge Canal after having part of the defensive nets caught in her propellers. (J. Revyn)

The problems experienced by the *Thetis* were avoided in the case of the scuttling of the similar 3,600-ton cruisers *Intrepid* and *Iphigenia* in the same canal. They entered without hindrance and completely blocked the access of German submarines to their base. (J. Revyn)

A German aerial view of the two cruisers *Intrepid* and *Iphigenia* shows how effective these blockships were at preventing access to the canal. By extreme good fortune the crews of both these ships escaped practically unharmed to be picked up by motor launches.

The submarine C-3 laden with ten tons of amatol was sunk by Lieutenant R.D. Sandford under the viaduct linking the mole to the shore. Some Germans came down to look at what they thought was a stranded submarine. Sandford set the fuse for five minutes and departed with his crew in their boat. The subsequent detonation sent about thirty yards of the causeway and most of the Germans sky-high! Lieutenant Sandford was awarded the Victoria Cross for this exploit but sadly within two years he had died of typhoid.

The final resting place of HMS *Vindictive*, here sunk as a blockship at Ostend. Again a fierce battle attended her arrival which merited the award of a further three Victoria Crosses. As he left the ship, William Bury realized, 'There was a fearful din on the upper deck, with machine-gun bullets as well as shrapnel; several of our people never got further than the escape doors.' She was later partially dismantled by the Germans and her hull was raised by the British after the war. Her bow remains today in a park at Ostend as a monument to a famous ship and her gallant crew.

Two officers and sixty-four men of the *Vindictive* were buried together in a single grave at St James's Cemetery, Dover, on 28 April 1918. The body of Admiral Keyes was later to join them. There is also a monument at Zeebrugge. (A.L.)

Early in the Second World War the Germans laid many magnetic mines in inshore waters, the destroyer HMS *Blanche* being lost off Margate to this cause on 13 November 1939. She was the first British destroyer to be lost in this later conflict, suffering one man killed and ten injured.

The *Blanche* was escorting the minelayer HMS *Adventure* (6,740 tons), which was the first to explode a mine. Although she survived, the cost in human life and suffering was much greater in her case, twelve men being killed and sixty-two wounded. Additionally, as the mine exploded beneath a fuel tank, heavy fuel oil was blasted right through the ship as high as the weather deck, covering everything and everyone in its path. (Gieves)

As a result of these casualties, attempts were made immediately to recover one of these new mines as ships were being sunk in channels already swept for moored mines. The minesweeper HMS *Mastiff* became a victim when trying to bring a mine to the surface in her trawl on 20 November 1939. HM Trawler *Cape Spartel* rescued the crew and four injured survivors were brought ashore by the Margate lifeboat. (Vicary)

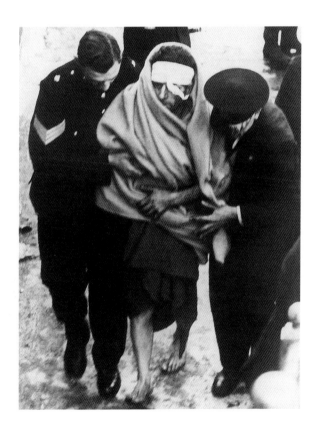

An injured survivor arrives ashore at Margate after he had 'got the hammer,' as those who suffered sinking by this new horror were described.

Three destroyers lost locally during the first year of the war. *Top:* HMS *Gipsy*, another victim of a magnetic mine, was sunk only about two cables' distance from Landguard point at Harwich on 21 November 1939. (*The Sphere*) *Centre:* HMS *Keith* lost with a large number of casualties while evacuating troops from Dunkirk on 1 June 1940. *Bottom:* HMS *Brazen*, which was sunk by air attack off Dover on 20 July 1940.

A further destroyer loss was the flotilla leader HMS *Codrington*, which was bombed and sunk in Dover Harbour a week after the sinking of the *Brazen*. German attacks on shipping in the Straits increased rapidly following the withdrawal from Dunkirk, causing the remaining warships to be removed from Dover Harbour. (Cribb)

The sunken HMS *Codrington* lies alongside the burning supply vessel *Sandhurst* in Dover Harbour after the raid of 27 July. Later the bow section of the destroyer was drawn up on to the beach where it remained for the rest of the war.

The French Navy also suffered severely at the time of Dunkirk. The destroyer *Bourrasque* (1,458 tons) is here shown sinking off Dunkirk after striking a mine while evacuating 700 troops on 30 May, 1940. Some fifty-six ratings were lost out of her complement of 159. Most of those aboard were saved by the French *Branlebas* and two British trawlers.

Bombed off Dunkirk on 21 May, the similar destroyer *L'Adroit* ended up ashore on the beach at Malo les Bains, where she was the target for further attacks. Her captain, an artillery specialist, and surviving crew then went ashore and fought in defence of the town.

A third ship of this class, the *Sirocco,* built in 1925, was torpedoed and sunk by a German MTB off Dunkirk on 31 May with the loss of a number of her crew.

This smaller French warship, *Chasseur 9,* also ended up as a wreck on the beach at Malo les Bains after suffering an air attack. It was this heroic ship and her crew that managed to rescue 154 men from the burning SS *Pavon* under a hail of machine-gun fire from German aircraft. Some nineteen French minesweepers and requisitioned trawlers were also lost at the time of the evacuation.

After 1941 there were few warship losses in the eastern Channel as the action moved elsewhere. Towards the end of the war casualties occurred again as streams of ships flowed in convoy to supply the armies in France following the D-Day invasion of Normandy. One tragic loss was the requisitioned cable ship *Alert*, which was carrying out cable repair work off North Foreland. She was either torpedoed or ran over an old mine, being lost with all hands, some sixty in total, on 25 February 1945. Another *Alert*, a Trinity House yacht of 777 grt, was mined and sunk off Dover on 15 April 1917.

This final picture from the warship section shows the remains of a Canadian wooden minesweeper which lies today at the site of Elmley Ferry on the Swale. There is a companion vessel nearby and both were intended for demolition years ago in Milton Creek but that work was never carried out. (A.L.)

two

Mercantile Victims of War

A significant and notorious loss of the First World War was the hospital ship *Anglia*, mined one mile east of the Folkestone gate of the Channel mine-barrage on 17 November 1915. In peacetime she had been operated by the London & North-Western Railway Company. (A. Vicary)

Over 130 men, mostly wounded soldiers, were drowned when the *Anglia* sank. This painting by W.H. Koek-Koek is perhaps a shade too dramatic, as contemporary photographs do not show the stern rising as high as this, but it gives a vivid impression of the occasion. A collier, the *Lusitania*, came to the aid of the *Anglia* but she also struck a mine and was lost, her crew having to look after themselves.

Another passenger vessel involved in the conflict was the SS *Brussels*, operated by the Great Eastern Railway on the Harwich-Hook of Holland service. While on a commercial voyage on 28 March 1915 the vessel was ordered to stop by a German submarine, but her master, Captain Fryatt, at first took avoiding action and then attempted to ram the U-boat. No further attempt to attack or arrest the *Brussels* was made on that day.

On 23 June 1916, the *Brussels* was making another regular homeward passage when she was intercepted by four German torpedo boats and escorted to Zeebrugge. Captain Fryatt was taken to Bruges and, after a show trial, was shot on 27 July 1916. An official German statement recorded that, 'Although he was not a member of the combatant force, he made an attempt to ram the submarine U-33 on the afternoon of 28 March 1915, near the Maas lightvessel.' Captain Fryatt's body was later brought back to Dover with a ceremonial procession in recognition of his valour.

The SS *Brussels* was kept at Zeebrugge by the Germans for a while as a submarine-depot ship but they later scuttled her off the end of the mole as part of the harbour defences. She was in that position when the Zeebrugge raid occurred. In the summer of 1919 she was raised in the salvage operations at the port, although she contained 1,000 tons of mud. Remarkably, she was repaired and later returned to service as the cattle carrier *Lady of Brussels*.

A third railway ferry to be sunk was the steamer *The Queen*, earlier pride of the Dover/ Folkestone-Calais route and the first cross-Channel steamer in the world to be fitted with turbine machinery. She was operating as a military transport between Folkestone and Boulogne, when boarded and sunk by gunfire on the night of 26 October 1916. Fortunately, the vessel had no troops aboard at the time. (Valentines)

The P&O liner *Moldavia* was a larger mercantile vessel-turned-warrior. While serving as an armed merchant cruiser she was torpedoed by UB-57 on 23 May 1918 off Eastbourne. More than fifty American troops aboard were unable to escape before the vessel sank. An earlier major loss by the P&O company was the 12,000-grt *Maloja*, mined off Dover with a large loss of life in February 1916. (Hughes & Son – via World Ship Society)

Many of the first mercantile losses of the Second World War were due to mines. One early victim was the Japanese motor vessel *Terukuni Maru*, also of 12,000 grt, which went down off Harwich on 21 November 1939 having almost completed her voyage from Yokohama to London. The header picture for this chapter shows the liner sinking. (World Ship Society)

Only three days before the loss of the *Terukuni Maru*, the smaller Dutch liner *Simon Bolivar* had struck two mines in the same region and sunk with more than eighty passengers and crew lost. The two crosses on the hull indicate where the mines exploded. She was bound for the West Indies from Amsterdam. (*The Sphere*)

Rescued members of the crew of the 8,400-grt *Simon Bolivar* gather ashore. (*The Sphere*)

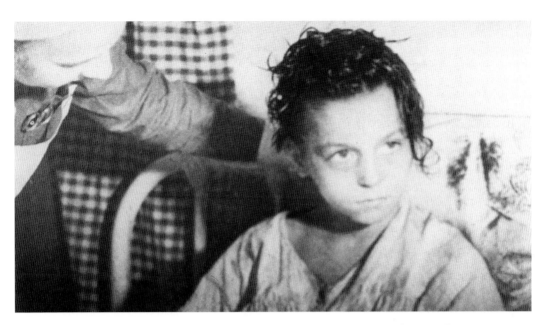

Christina Wensvoort was a small Dutch girl who survived the disaster. She was taken to a London hospital for treatment. There was a large number of children aboard, no doubt fleeing the Netherlands as war drew nearer. One little boy lost both his parents when the ship sank. (*The Sphere*)

Another Dutch liner, the *Spaarndam* of the Holland–America Line, was lost in this early period. Inward-bound from Tampico, the 9,000-grt vessel struck a mine east-north-east of the Tongue lightship about ten miles off Margate on 27 November 1939. On this occasion only seven lives were lost. (World Ship Society)

Above: General cargo ships fared no better than passenger liners and no nationality was protected. The Italian *Grazia* is here shown capsized and sinking seven miles off Margate on 19 November 1939. The survivors of the crew abandoned ship in their boat and were picked up.

Above: Going down on an even keel is the British steamer *Blackhill*, mined on the previous day less than a mile from the Long Sand Head buoy off Harwich. She was bound for the river Tees with 3,650 tons of iron ore but never reached there. Fortunately, only one of her crew was lost.

Opposite above: Tugs and salvors fight to save the Dutch Shell oil tanker *Phobos*, victim of a mine off Deal on 20 March 1940. The ship had a cargo of 9,600 tons of crude oil and was struck just forward of the bridge on the starboard side. The master and fifty-one crew were taken off, the first officer being killed. After a time, the tugs attending brought the ingress of water under control. Although not of the highest quality, this photograph captures some of the atmosphere of the occasion.

Above: The explosion damage to the bridge of the tanker *Phobos* is evident in this later view. After the ship was righted, pumping was maintained and a number of the officers were able to rejoin her. On 22 March the tanker left for Shell Haven in the Thames in tow of tugs. She had lost about 1,500 tons of oil from striking the mine but fortunately there was no major fire.

Two days before the incident involving the *Phobos*, an Italian vessel, the *Tina Primo*, had fared worse some two miles to the north of the position of the tanker. The 4,800-grt ship, which was on a voyage from Rotterdam to Genoa in ballast, broke in half amidships and sank relatively slowly. Only one member of the crew was lost. Her bell was found recently by divers. (Arthur Taylor)

On the day the *Phobos* struck the mine, the SS *Barn Hill* was inward bound along the Channel from Halifax, Nova Scotia, with a general cargo destined for London. Off Beachy Head she became the victim of a concentrated air attack which left her a blazing wreck. The Eastbourne lifeboat *Jane Holland* was called out to rescue her crew and took ten men off, but as the ship burned ever more fiercely, it was found that her master had been blown from the bridge on to the forecastle and lay there seriously injured. The *Jane Holland* returned and put two courageous crewmen on the forward end where, despite flames, smoke and sparks, they got the injured man into the lifeboat and gained the Bronze Medal in the process. The *Barn Hill* drifted ashore and became a total wreck.

A shipwrecked crew is brought ashore at Margate. Men from the SS *Dalryan* climb the ladder on the stone pier after being saved by the lifeboat *The Lord Southborough (Civil Service No. 1)*.

Crew members of the Margate lifeboat relax outside their boathouse between Battle of Britain calls, sporting their latest headgear. The boat was also provided with a rifle to repel the enemy. Coxswain Ted Parker is in the foreground on the left, while the crew members are Dennis Price, Arthur Ladd, Harry Sandwell, Hon. Sec. A.C. Robinson, Arthur 'Buller' Morris, Harry Parker (bowman), Ernie Barrs (mechanic), Tom Campany and Alf Lacey (assistant mechanic).

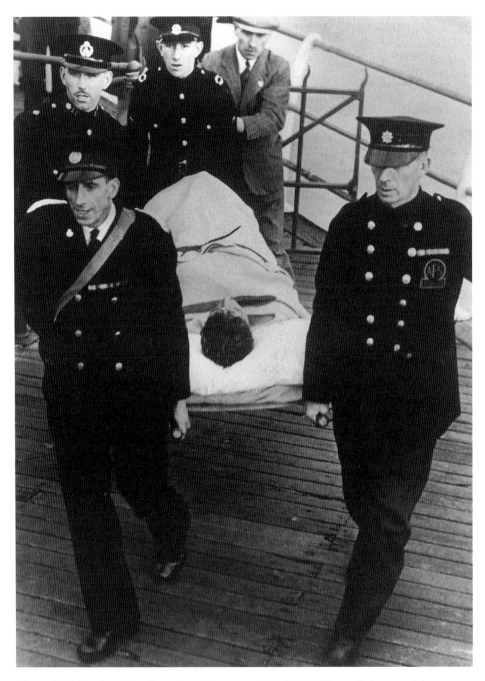

Above: An injured survivor from the minesweeper HMS *Mastiff* is carried to a waiting ambulance at Margate. Often these mine explosions caused severe injuries to the legs of victims due to the violent upward movement of the deck.

Opposite: The French coast suffered from its share of mines also, up to the time of the retreat from Dunkirk. The 216-grt tug *Hercule* was sunk by the usual magnetic variety to the east of Calais on 20 May 1940. After this date air attacks prevailed. (Calais War Museum)

French merchant ships lost between Boulogne and Dunkirk at the time of the evacuation in the spring of 1940:

Name	GRT	Place	Cause	Date
Ophelie (tanker)	6,477	Off Boulogne	Air attack	20/5/1940
Hercule (tug)	216	East of Calais	Mine	20/5/1940
Portrieux	2,257	Off Gravelines	Air attack	22/5/1940
Pavon	4,128	Near Oye Plage	Air attack	22/5/1940
Aden	8,033	Dunkirk	Air attack	27/5/1940
Monique Schiaffino	3,236	Dunkirk	Air attack	29/5/1940
Saint Octave	5,099	Dunkirk	Scuttled	End May 1940
Ceres	3,073	Dunkirk	Air attack	29/5/1940
Mars	721	Dunkirk	Air attack	29/5/1940
Ain-el-Turk	2,008	Dunkirk	Air attack	31/5/1940
Cote d'Azur (ferry) ★	3,047	Dunkirk	Air attack	27/5/1940
Le Puissant (tug)	245	Dunkirk	Air attack	31/5/1940
Costaud (tug)	140	Dunkirk	Air attack	31/5/1940
Adjader (tug)	414	Dunkirk	Air attack	31/5/1940
Douaisien	2,954	Off Dunkirk	Mine	1/6/1940
Saint Camille	3,274	Dunkirk	Mine	2/6/1940
Salome	–	Dunkirk	Scuttled	3/6/1940
Rouen	1,882	Dunkirk	Air attack	12/6/1940
Cap Tafelneh	2,300	Dunkirk	Air attack	12/6/1940
Vauban (tug)	–	Dunkirk	–	6/1940
Rennes	771	Dunkirk	–	–
Laplace (tug)	–	–	–	–
Lavoisier (tug)	–	–	–	–
Jean Millot (tug)	180	–	–	–

★The *Cote d'Azur* was raised by the Germans in 1941 and converted to a minelayer for use in the Baltic, where she disappeared in 1944, either sunk or scuttled in the region of Stettin.

The worst French merchant casualty at the time of Dunkirk was the SS *Pavon*, owned by Compagnie de Navigation d'Orbigny. This ship, commanded by Captain Jean Perdrault, was diverted to pick up several hundred disarmed Dutch soldiers from Dunkirk on 20 May 1940. She eventually left safely at 10 p.m. with close to 1,000 men aboard, including a few German prisoners, but some of the 180 Stukas which had earlier attacked the town returned in the light of the full moon. (World Ship Society)

As the *Pavon* was approaching Calais the aircraft dived towards her, releasing 50kg bombs. She was instantly hit by two in No.3 hold where men were reclining on bales of the cotton cargo. Fire rapidly developed and many jumped into the sea, where fortunately rescue craft were at hand. Captain Perdrault drove the ship ashore on the beach near the Walde lighthouse at Hemmes-de-Marck, where she was completely burned out. The official Dutch record gave the number lost as 152. (Calais War Museum)

Much has previously been written about British ships lost at Dunkirk. The one example chosen here is the *Queen of the Channel*, bombed by an isolated aircraft when leaving laden with troops on 28 May 1940. Nearly everyone aboard was safely taken aboard the store ship *Dorrien Rose* and brought to Dover, having fared better than those aboard the *Pavon*.

A postscript to Dunkirk. The beaches are empty except for the refuse of war. A number of Thames barges never came back, including *Ethel Everard, Royalty, Lark, Aidie, Doris* and *Duchess*. The wreck of the Gaselee tug *Fossa* lies in the background on the left.

Fewer ships were mined after the withdrawal from Dunkirk, but one unlucky vessel was the *Empire Commerce,* loaded with 5,400 tons of pulpwood from Canada. She struck a mine at the entrance to the Thames on 9 June 1940 and was put ashore on the Margate Sand to prevent her from sinking, but she refloated herself in fog after being abandoned. Tugs searched for her and eventually towed her to London, only her cargo keeping her afloat. She is shown here under her earlier name of *Goodleigh.* (A. Duncan)

The officers of the *Empire Commerce* appear cheerful in spite of the difficulties they are about to face. They are Captain Horace 'Jim' Miller (seated) and, from left to right: first officer John Greene, the second officer, and finally third mate Norman James. (Norman James)

Until the Second World War, lightvessels, being seamarks valuable to all seafarers, were regarded as neutral. As can be seen from the following table, this was not the case in the last conflict, when many were attacked. Losses are highlighted in grey. (A.L.)

Lightvessels lost in the Narrow Seas 1877–1954:

Vessel	Station	Cause of Loss	Date	Comments
No.5	Tongue	Collision	12/7/1877	Colliding vessel SS *Rhine*
No.49	Kentish Knock	Collision	1/12/1886	Colliding vessel *Palawan*
No.22	–	Wrecked at Seaford	10/1894	Broke adrift while on tow
No.24	Dover Pier Works	Collision	12/11/1901	Colliding vessel SS *Le Nord*
No.41	Dover Pier Works	Collision	10/5/1902	Colliding vessel SS *Calchas*
No.38	Gull	Collision	17/3/1929	Colliding vessel SS *City of York*. Vessel raised and repaired
	Dyck	Enemy action	25/5/1940	French lightvessel
No.54	East Goodwin	Enemy action	18/7/1940	Unmanned
No.26	South Falls war station	Unknown	24/7/1940	Unmanned float
No.75	South Folkestone Gate	Bombed	14/8/1940	Two crew lost
No.52	Trinity war station	Unknown	1/10/1940	–
No.69	South Goodwin	Unknown	25/11/1940	Unmanned; Disappeared
No.60	East Oaze	Bombed	1/11/1940	Seven crew lost
No.20	Lydd war station	Unknown	7/1/1941	Unmanned float
No.14	F. Beachy Head	Foundered	13/10/1944	Unmanned
No.46	H. Beachy Head	Foundered	13/10/1944	Unmanned
No.90	South Goodwin	Wrecked in storm	27/11/1954	Seven crew lost

The badly damaged bow of lightvessel No.38. This did not occur as a result of an enemy attack, but was caused by the Italian vessel SS *Ernani* colliding with her on the Brake station on 16 January 1940. The crew abandoned her in atrocious weather and were lucky to be saved. The lightship remained afloat but was withdrawn. Since that time a buoy has marked the Brake Sand. (*The Sphere*)

After Dunkirk the coastal ships travelling in convoy were mauled very badly by German bombers. Most of these ships were carrying coal to south-coast power stations. Westbound convoy CW08 of late July 1940 lost nine ships out of twenty-one, with a further four badly damaged. The collier *Henry Moon* belonging to one of the local power authorities was sunk off Folkestone. (World Ship Society)

Above: During the same attack Everard's *Summity* was also struck by a bomb, but in her case the blast was reduced somewhat by her cement cargo, and, although leaking badly, her master managed to beach her under Shakespeare Cliff at Dover. She was subsequently refloated, repaired and returned to service, ultimately surviving the war to bring coal to Margate in later years. (F.T. Everard)

Opposite below: SS *Grønland*, the commodore's vessel damaged in the above convoy, was sunk in Dover Harbour by aerial bombardment on 29 July 1940. (World Ship Society)

A list of ships comprising convoy CW08 with details of their fortunes. They were escorted by the armed trawlers *Arctic Pioneer*, *Drangey* and *Amethyst*. Very soon after this the convoys ceased running as the risks were too high and they only commenced again after D-Day. (A.L.)

Ships Comprising Convoy CW8 of late July 1940:

Vessel	GRT	Voyage	Cargo	Fate
Broadhurst	1,013	Seaham for Shoreham	Coal	Sunk by E-boat fourteen miles south-west of Shoreham 26/7/1940
Corhaven	991	Tyne for Portsmouth	Coal	Sunk by air attack off Dover
Grønland	1,264	Blyth for Plymouth	Coal	Damaged
Henry Moon	1,091	Burntisland for Shoreham	Coal	Sunk by air attack two miles off Folkestone 25/7/1940
Hodder	1,016	Blyth for Cowes	Coal	Damaged
Leo	1,140	Seaham for Portsmouth	Coal	Sunk by air attack off Dover
London Trader	646	Tyne for Shoreham	Coal	Sunk by air attack thirteen miles south-west of Shoreham 26/7/1940
Lulonga	821	Goole for Shoreham	Ballast	Sunk by air attack fifteen miles south of Shoreham 26/7/1940
Newminster	804	Seaham for Portsmouth	Coal	Damaged
Polgrange	804	Blyth for Cowes	Coal	Sunk by air attack off Dover
Portslade	1,091	Sunderland for Shoreham	Coal	Sunk by air attack four to five miles north-east of Dungeness 25/7/1940
Summity	554	London for Plymouth	Cement	damaged, beached at Dover
Tamworth	1,332	Blyth for Southampton	Coal	Damaged
Mistley	487	For Weymouth	Coal	Survived
Jolly Nights	351	For Devonport	General	Survived
Dominence	263	For Charlestown	Cement	Survived
Surte (Du.)	244	For Southampton	General	Survived
Balder (Nor.)	1,129	–	–	Survived
Sanfry	946	For Shoreham	Coal	Survived
Arthur Wright	1,091	For Shoreham	Coal	Survived
British Scout	1,507	–	–	Survived

Once shipping movements recommenced after the D-Day landings, further casualties occurred. The Dutch Shell tanker *Liseta* was torpedoed near the stern off Margate on 15 February 1945. Fortunately, her cargo of gasoline was unaffected. Her forward part remained afloat but the stern broke away and sank. The forepart was salvaged and taken to London. Later it is believed a new stern was constructed and the vessel re-entered service. (Norman Cavell)

The sailing trawler *Volante* was the peacetime victim of a wartime mine. Fishing near the Kentish Knock on 12 October 1950, she hauled up a mine in her trawl which exploded directly beneath the ship. Her crew of three were lucky to survive and, finding their small ship's boat intact, pulled to the Tongue lightvessel from where the Ramsgate lifeboat brought them ashore. (Frank Boxall)

three

Saga of Collisions

Numerous collisions have occurred in the river Thames over the years, but fortunately few passenger vessels have been involved. Two of these rare events are recorded on this page. On 1 July 1852 the Ramsgate paddle steamer *Duchess of Kent* was run down off Northfleet Point by the general steam vessel *Ravensbourne* on passage from London to Antwerp. The pleasure steamer sank but most of those aboard were rescued by the other craft in the vicinity. (*Illustrated London News*)

This was not the case with the sinking of the *Princess Alice* after a collision with the collier SS *Bywell Castle* off Margaret Ness on 3 September 1878. The crowded pleasure steamer went down very quickly, taking some 640 passengers with her, making this the second worst accident on the waters of south-east England after the explosion aboard the *Bulwark*. This engraving shows the raising of the bow section of the *Princess Alice*.

A dramatic collision had also occurred off Dover on 17 February 1876, although the loss of life was much less. Just after leaving the harbour and destined for Bombay, the SS *Strathclyde* was in collision with the German steamer *Franconia*, the former being holed amidships in the port side. The *Strathclyde* sank rapidly in the heavy swell, drowning thirty-eight of the seventy passengers and crew aboard.

The *Franconia* backs away after sinking the *Strathclyde*. A number of important German vessels were to be involved in accidents in the eastern Channel in the late Victorian years.

Only two years later, the Hamburg–America steamer *Pommerania* of 3,400 grt, belonging to the same owners as the *Franconia*, sank off Dover after collision with the iron barque *Moel Eilian*. It was about midnight on 14 November 1878 when the collision occurred, the *Pommerania* remaining afloat for about twenty minutes. This delay encouraged passengers to go below for their valuables and forty-eight were lost when the vessel suddenly sank. (World Ship Society)

The bows of the *Moel Eilian* were so badly damaged that she was fortunate to reach Dover. Most of the survivors from the *Pommerania* were picked up by the SS *Glengarry*. (*Illustrated London News*)

A third major casualty in the Dover area was the Holland–America emigrant steamer
W.A. Scholten, which struck the collier *Rosa Mary* lying at anchor four miles east of the port on
19 November 1887. Once again the collision occurred at night. The Dutch vessel quickly
developed a list which prevented her launching all her boats. (Netherlands Historich Scheepvaart
Museum, Amsterdam)

A dramatic reconstruction of the sinking of the *W.A. Scholten* drawn from the evidence of a
survivor. This was the most costly accident of the three Dover Straits collisions here described, as
132 were lost out of the 210 aboard, including the master, Captain J.H. Taat. (*The Graphic*)

A notable collision of the early twentieth century was between Laeisz's nitrate clipper *Pisagua* and the P&O Liner *Oceana*, resulting in the sinking of the latter off Eastbourne on 15 March 1912, close to the date of the loss of SS *Titanic*. Although fortunately the loss of life was small, considerable publicity was attached to this event as the *Oceana* had almost £750,000 in gold and silver bullion aboard. Most of this was soon recovered in an epic salvage operation. (World Ship Society)

One notable survivor from the *Oceana* was the ship's cat, whose name unfortunately is not known. (Campbell McCutcheon collection)

Right: As permanently anchored vessels and bright red in colour, lightships should have been easily avoided, especially as they were situated close to sandbanks. Records show, however, that collisions with these vessels were numerous, although not many were sunk. A vessel moored in the Gull Stream off Ramsgate was unlucky, for it was struck at night in fog and sunk by a large steamer on 17 March 1929.

Below: Skipper Harry Meakins of the Deal boat Lady Beatty, which carried out service visits to the Goodwins' lightvessels, was requested by Trinity House to mark the position of the sunken vessel until a replacement could be obtained. He is shown here on the left, with his crew: Charlie Pritchard, Edward Griggs, Tommy Baker, 'Dick' Brown and Dave Pritchard. They had only a portable signal from a sailing ship and a bell to warn approaching ships of the danger.

This picture graphically shows the damage caused by the impact of the bows of the 7,800-grt Ellerman steamer *City of York*. Although the Gull lightvessel sank very quickly, amazingly six of the crew escaped, only the master, Captain Williams, being lost. A few months later, vessel No.38 was raised and rebuilt for further service. Surprisingly, she still survives to this day as a hulk on the foreshore at Grays in Essex.

This illustration of the SS *City of York* shows her vertical stem, which must have struck the lightship with great force. A craft of lesser strength would probably have been cut completely in two. (A. Duncan)

A further danger of navigating in shallow waters is the possibility of striking submerged wreckage. The coaster SS *Solway Firth* suffered this misfortune in the early days of November 1928. Her master found her suddenly sinking off Margate in three fathoms, leaving the crew no option but to abandon ship in their lifeboat. They remained secured to the wreck until visibility cleared some six hours later, when they were found by a passing ship, none the worse for their experience.

After the Belgian steamer *Flandres* sank due to a collision with the SS *Kabalo* in the Downs in February 1940, her wreck remained in the fairway. Soon afterwards, in a period of limited visibility, the SS *Fluor* ran on to the remains of the *Flandres* and it was some time before she could get free. When work commenced to demolish the wreck of the *Flandres* after the war, an accidental explosion of the demolition charge killed five ratings from HMS *Lundy*. (Norman Cavell)

When tankers were victims of a collision, the result could be catastrophic. The T2 tanker *Newhall Hills* lost her bow completely in such an incident east of the Goodwin Sands on 24 May 1947. Although she suffered an explosion and fire, only one man was lost. The tugs *Gondia, Kenia* and *Lady Brassey* towed the vessel stern-first to Sheerness and then London. (John G. Callis)

On 31 January 1948 the Elder Dempster freighter *Freetown* was proceeding up the river Thames when she ran aground in Northfleet Hope. Refloated without damage by tugs, she continued upriver the next day, but was then unfortunately in collision with two colliers, the *Corcrest* and *Yewcrest* at Erith. The former suffered the damage to her bow, shown here, and two of her crew lost their lives. (Campbell McCutcheon collection)

Another vessel to lose her bow was the war-built Liberty ship *Western Farmer*, which collided with the tanker *Bjorgholm* on 20 August 1952 eighteen miles east-south-east of Ramsgate. This time the laden Norwegian tanker survived and it was the coal-carrying dry-cargo ship which broke in half. The stern of the *Western Farmer* was eventually beached near Calais by French tugs. It was later taken to Dunkirk for discharge of the cargo. (Chris Fright)

Coxswain Douglas Kirkaldie and the crew of the Ramsgate lifeboat *Prudential* rescued the crew of the *Western Farmer* after it broke in half while they were standing by. He gained a Bronze Medal from the RNLI for this service. Later he was presented with a plaque by the United States Seafarers' Union, as shown in this photograph. Kirkaldie stands at the left and coxswain John Walker of the Dover lifeboat, who also received a plaque, stands second from right. (Sunbeam Photo Ltd)

Left: There follows a selection of English Channel collision victims taken from the fifties. The *Baron Douglas*, in front, lies low in the water after being struck by the Yugoslav steamer *Korenica* early on 14 June 1952 off Hastings. Eastbourne, Hastings and Dungeness lifeboats all went to her and took off some crew. The vessel was beached to save her from sinking. (John Reynolds)

Below: Hit in nearly the same place on the starboard side on 21 March 1952 by the British steamer *Benwyvis* in fog, the Spanish SS *Guecho* takes assistance from tugs four miles south-east of Dover Harbour. The *Guecho* was brought into that port and temporarily repaired to allow her to continue to Antwerp, her original destination. (Lambert Weston)

Above: Serious damage is apparent on the starboard bow of the Dutch motor vessel *Prins Alexander* following her encounter with the Norwegian steamer *N.O. Rogenaes* on 10 July 1952. In the collision off the Sandettie Bank, a hole about 30ft long and 8ft high was torn in the side of the Dutch ship. She was also brought into Dover Harbour for repairs. (G.W. Jezard)

Right: All four ships on these two pages suffered collision damage on the starboard side forward and all survived their ordeal. This last example is the French steamer *Dione*, crippled by contact with the *Michael C* five miles east of the South Foreland on 8 July 1956. The SS *Dione* was towed to Calais stern-first by the Dover tugs with the lifeboat in attendance. (*Planet News*)

Despite increasingly accurate aids to navigation, lightships are still hit, although the frequency is much less than a hundred years ago. Such an event was a terrifying experience for the crew because they could do little to avoid the collision, except pay out more cable. On 28 June 1981, lightvessel No.21 at the Varne suffered the peculiar calamity of having a tug pass down one side and its tow, a large ore-carrier, hit the other. (Fotoflite, Ashford)

The 18,000-grt vessel *Ore Meteor* was bound for the ship-breakers in tow of the tug *Suzanne*. Considering the size of its assailant, the Varne lightship was lucky to escape with a broken foremast and smashed lantern. It was surprising also that there were no injuries to the crew. (World Ship Society)

Ferries have not been spared entirely from collisions, but these have been infrequent compared to the number of Channel or North Sea crossings they make. In spite of this rarity, there have been several instances of two ferries colliding, including that involving the Townsend Thoresen-owned *European Gateway* and the *Speedlink Vanguard* off Harwich on 19 December 1982. The *European Gateway* capsized as a consequence and settled on the sea bed with six people lost. (World Ship Society)

The *Speedlink Vanguard* shown in calmer weather. A gale was blowing at the time of the collision and darkness prevailed, conditions which made it very difficult for the Harwich pilot boats to effect a rescue while the *Dana Futura* stood by as command ship. The Trinity House launches *Valour* and *Patrol* rescued forty-seven people in total from the *European Gateway*, their crews later receiving Bronze Medals from the RNLI. (*Trinity House Gazette*)

There was a further incident of a similar type involving two train ferries when, on 1 May 1987, the French *St Eloi* and the British *Cambridge Ferry* collided in fog just outside the western entrance of Dover Harbour. (A. Duncan)

The *Cambridge Ferry* suffered severe damage to her bows but injuries were fortunately few among the passengers. Particular concern was expressed when this accident happened as such a short time had elapsed since the capsize of the *Herald of Free Enterprise* at Zeebrugge. (Maritime and Coastguard Agency)

If one of the ships sank following a collision there was often concern about consequent pollution. One particular case was the French ro-ro vessel *Mont Louis*, which sank about twelve miles off Ostend after collision with the Sheerness ferry *Olau Britannia* on 25 August 1984. The *Mont Louis* was carrying 450 tons of uranium salts for conversion to enriched uranium for power station use. (World Ship Society)

The *Mont Louis* broke into two pieces in the stormy seas following her sinking, but in spite of this salvagers recovered all the drums of uranium compounds. (Fotoflite, Ashford)

The worst cases of pollution are associated with oil tankers and fortunately no really large vessel has sunk in the Narrow Seas. One event that could have had a very serious outcome was the collision between the fully-laden 67,200-grt tanker *Skyron*, above, and the Polish cargo vessel *Hel* twenty miles east of Ramsgate on 30 May 1987. It was indeed fortunate that the *Skyron* struck the *Hel*, rather than the other way around, because the fire that developed was limited to the paint store in the bow of the tanker and did not spread to the cargo. (Fotoflite, Ashford)

The ore/oil-carrier *Bona Fulmar* also had a lucky escape when it was struck by the Mexican chemical tanker M/V *Teoatl* in dense fog near the northern end of the Channel separation zone on 18 January 1997. The *Bona Fulmar* lost about 5,000 tons of unleaded gasoline through the breach in her side. Amazingly, no fire developed but later it rained gasoline over the Midlands and East Anglia.

The very latest and most spectacular of these events occurred when the Norwegian car-carrier *Tricolor* was struck by the container ship *Kariba* in the early hours of 14 December 2002. After the accident, the car-carrier rolled over and sank, taking to the bottom £30 million-worth of luxury cars. As is apparent from this photograph, the waters of the Channel are relatively shallow and the starboard side of the wreck initially dried at low tide, making it a hazard to navigation. (Channel Photography)

The 50,000-grt *Tricolor* was a big ship even by modern standards and a closely similar vessel, the *Takara,* is shown here to better illustrate the type involved. She was the largest ship ever lost in the area of water covered by this book, and the cutting up and salvage of the wreck by Smit-Tak has been one of the largest and most costly of its kind. (A.L.)

Not only was the sinking of the *Tricolor* with its 2,862 BMW, Saab and Volvo cars a notorious event, but other collisions with the sunken wreck followed in a manner reminiscent of the ships that tragically hit the *Texaco Caribbean* in 1971. This illustration shows the *Nicola* perched high and dry on the *Tricolor* as night falls on 16 December. On 1 January 2003 the Turkish tanker *Vicky* loaded with 70,000 tons of diesel oil also struck the *Tricolor,* damaging her tanks and creating some pollution. (Maritime and Coastguard Agency – Crown Copywrite)

four

Ships Ashore

The earliest vessel lost by stranding illustrated in this work is the famous Dutch East Indiaman *Amsterdam*. She was run ashore by a mutinous crew at Bulverhythe, near Hastings, on 26 January 1749 while on her maiden voyage from Amsterdam to Java. Fortunately, the hull of this important ship has been preserved along with a considerable number of artefacts, and salvage continues. A replica of the ship is located at Amsterdam. (Peter Marsden, Shipwreck Heritage Centre, Hastings)

Although a number of sailing Indiamen were wrecked on the coasts of south-east England, relatively few contemporary illustrations are available. This rare view shows salvage work on the West Indiaman *Active*, which together with the *Hindostan* of the East India Company was wrecked near Margate on 10/11 January 1803.

Right: A twelve-pound gun taken from the wreck site of the *Hindostan* bears the date 1790. The ship carried thirty guns altogether. This one is displayed at the Ramsgate Maritime Museum. (A.L.)

Below: In 1809, two more East Indiamen, the *Admiral Gardner* and the *Britannia*, were wrecked on the Goodwin Sands in a gale. The first of these vessels has also yielded a number of important artefacts. This contemporary painting shows the *Britannia* passing through the Downs.

Above: The worst loss of life due to stranding in this region occurred when, on 23 November 1802, the Dutch troopship *Vryheid* drove ashore at Dymchurch in a tremendous gale. Although wrecked close to land, 454 of those aboard were drowned in the disaster, which was in some part attributed to the master's reluctance to take a pilot. Only eighteen were saved. The *Vryheid* was previously the British East Indiaman *Melville Castle*. (Dutch engraving)

Opposite: Details of a typical sale of effects at Whitstable resulting from a shipwreck. These sales were commonplace in the nineteenth century, when wrecks were all too frequent, especially in wintertime. (Ramsgate Maritime Museum)

A CATALOGUE

OF

Damaged Sugar and Molasses,

AND

Empty Hogsheads,

SAVED FROM

The Ship "FORTITUDE"

Captain JOHN STAFFORD;

TO BE

SOLD by AUCTION,

BY

WILLIAM WHORLOW,

FOR ACCOUNT OF THE UNDERWRITERS,

At 12 o'Clock at Noon,

On MONDAY, the 4th of NOVEMBER, 1816,

AT

WHITSTABLE.

Conditions of Sale.

I.—The highest bidder to be the purchaser, who shall declare his or her name, and give in his or her place of residence, and immediately pay a deposit of £25 per cent on each lot, as part of payment.

II.—The lots to be taken away as they now lay lotted out, with all faults at the purchaser's expence, within seven days after the sale is ended, the remainder of the purchase money together with 2½ per cent on each lot to the broker, for lot money, first being paid.

III.—If any lot or lots remain uncleared after the time above limited, the deposit money shall be forfeited to the present proprietors, who shall not be liable to be sued for the same, either in law or in equity. The goods to be resold by public or private sale, and the deficiency, if any, by such resale, shall be made good by the defaulters, who shall be answerable for interest of money, risk of fire, and every expence arising in consequence of not complying with the conditions.

IV.—If any disputes arise at the sale between the bidders, the lot or lots in dispute shall be put up again immediately.

WITHERDEN, PRINTER, MARINE PARADE, MARGATE.

Above: Further details of items to be sold from the wreck of the 370-ton-ship *Fortitude.* (Ramsgate Maritime Museum)

Opposite below: Another stranding of some consequence was that of the *Earl of Eglinton* in St Margaret's Bay on 29 January 1860. The 1,275-grt ship was outward bound from London to Calcutta. Her master had not agreed terms with a pilot, and having passed Dover, was driven back to ground on the foreshore opposite what is now the Coastguard pub. In contrast to the *Vryheid*, however, there was only one fatality, that occurring during the removal of the cargo. (*Bygone Kent,* 1986)

Above: A further wreck of an East Indiaman was that of the *Tigress,* west of Shakespeare Cliff at Dover in February 1849. Her valuable cargo drew a large crowd who soon broached casks of rum as they floated ashore. 'A disgusting scene of drunkenness ensued – men, women and children lying on the beach, huddled together in the worst state of intoxication, so that many of them were nearly drowned by the rising of the tide.' (*Illustrated London News*)

THE *EARL OF EGLINTON*
FOR THE BENEFIT OF THE UNDERWRITERS
TO BE SOLD BY AUCTION BY
MR. THOMAS ROBINSON

On Thursday 16th February 1860 at one o'clock in the afternoon on the spot the ship *Earl of Eglinton* of Glasgow, 1275 tons register, J.N. Wandrop, Master, as she now lies stranded at St. Margaret's Bay near the South Foreland together with such portion of her cargo as may remain in her which originally consisted of calico, dyed cottons, linen bale goods, copper wire, government stores and other valuable goods and which are to be salvaged by the purchaser and delivered to the Receivers of Wreck in the neighbourhood for which salvage will be paid at the rate of 40%.

    After which will be sold in separate lots such portion of the ship's material, tackle and apparel, as are now lying at St. Margaret's Bay. For particulars apply to Messrs. Latham and Co., Lloyds agents for Dover, to Captain E.B. Knott R.N. special agent for Lloyds Deal, or to Mr. Thomas Robinson, auctioneer, Dover

This is a peculiar case of a deliberate stranding. When smuggling was at its height in the early nineteenth century, many Coast Blockade, later coastguard, stations were established along the coast. While most were buildings, two consisted of beached vessels, the brig *Pelter* at Copt Point, Folkestone and the sloop *Enchantress*, illustrated in this engraving, which resided at Rye Old Harbour between 1817 and 1831.

The Downs off Deal provided shelter for many vessels during south-westerly gales, but if the wind suddenly swung to north-east they were trapped on a lee shore and over the years numerous vessels were lost in this way. One of the worst occasions was in November 1877, when the coast was littered with dozens of wrecks, including the *Star of the Ocean* shown here near Kingsdown. (W.H. Franklin)

> But the evening closed on a conquered sea, and masts where
>   never a sailor clings;
> And they ran to the end of the Ramsgate Pier, to see the prize
>   that the lifeboat brings.
> It isn't in money or gold that's paid the terrible debt of the
>   enemy sea,
> But flesh and blood of a shipwrecked crew is a richer reward,
>   you'll all agree.
> Many a ship, as the year rolls on, with skipper and pilot, and
>   faithful hands,
> Will sail from home on a winter sea, and drift to death upon
>   Goodwin Sands.
> But when the plea for the lifeboat comes there'll not be many
>   To grudge relief
> To the men who answered to duty's call, and stood by the
>   Wreck of the *Indian Chief*.
>
> "Punch," January 22, 1881

Most famous of all ships stranded off shore in south-east England is the *Indian Chief*, wrecked on the Long Sand on 6 January 1881. The story of the incredible rescue and the award by the RNLI of its Gold Medal to Charles Fish, coxswain of the Ramsgate lifeboat *Bradford*, and eighteen Silver Medals to the crews of the lifeboat and tug *Vulcan* received great publicity. The author of this poem should perhaps have known better than to place the casualty on the Goodwin Sands, but others have made the same mistake. (*Punch*, 22 January 1881)

While some publicized the wreck of the *Indian Chief* in words, others celebrated the event in pictures. William Broome (1838-1892) was living in Ramsgate at the time, and, having already established himself as a marine painter, went on to portray the rescue from a large number of angles. These paintings were largely sold to raise funds for the RNLI. The subject was so popular that other painters produced similar works. (Ramsgate Maritime Museum)

Returning to the coast, the populace of Folkestone and Hythe witnessed a number of wrecks in the latter part of the nineteenth century. When the iron ship *Plassey* stranded at Seabrook in February 1883, she appeared sound enough to be refloated and salvors remained aboard her. (Mr Cheeseman)

Yet, as in so many cases, the arrival of a further gale within a week reduced the *Plassey* to a mass of broken wreckage and caused one of the salvors to lose his life.

A further and more famous wreck occurred in the same place in stormy conditions on
11 November 1891. The 2,033-grt Glasgow sailing ship *Benvenue* was under tow near Folkestone
at the start of her passage to Sydney, Australia. In the hurricane conditions prevailing she broke
away and struck bottom about 300 yards from shore at Seabrook. There followed frantic and
arduous attempts to rescue the crew by rocket line and by lifeboat, which went on for some
considerable time, but eventually the Hythe lifeboat was successful. (*Illustrated London News*)

A poem written in honour of the fishermen who made up the greater part of the Hythe lifeboat crew on the final attempt to take twenty-seven survivors off the wreck. Coxswain Laurence Hennesey and assistant coxswain Albert Sadler both gained RNLI Silver Medals for their courage and endurance on this occasion.

'The Wreck of the Benvenue', a fisherman's story. By Hal Berte.

> *Yes, sir, we're only fisherfolk, a rough and ready sort,*
> *Whose simple lives are mostly spent in bringing fish to port;*
> *We're not exactly lifeboat men, but still we do our share,*
> *And when there's volunteers required you'll always find us there.*
> *Seen wrecks? Well, yes, as boy and man I guess I've seen a few,*
> *For more than once our fishermen have made the lifeboat's crew;*
> *And when the* Benvenue *was wrecked with thirty souls or more,*
> *The Folkestone fishermen it was who brought her crew ashore.*
>
> *I've seen a few November gales, and pretty stiff ones, too,*
> *But never aught to equal that in which the* Benvenue
> *was wrecked and sunk off Sandgate here within the sight of land,*
> *With crowds of people looking on, who could not lend a hand.*
> *Her masts above the angry sea alone remained and there*
> *We saw her crew all huddled up, and breathed a fervent prayer*
> *That she might last till help arrived — that help we wished to give*
> *But could not, for in such a sea `twas plain no craft could live.*
>
> *We saw the lifeboat launched and then a sight I shan't forget,*
> *One awful wave, a piercing cry, 'My God, the boat's upset!'*
> *A fearful fight for life, and then the awful shout 'One's lost!'*
> *But yonder, crew, they must be saved no matter what it cost.*
> *Time after time, with rockets then to reach the wreck they tried,*
> *But not a rope could stand the stress of such a wind and tide.*
> *The hours went on, the storm still raged, the moon rose in the sky,*
> *And now there seemed but little else than leave them there to die.*
>
> *Nay! not while British hearts are made of sterling bulldog stuff.*
> *'A crew — who'll man the boat again?' answered a fisher bluff —*
> *'The fishermen of Folkestone will, we only want the word.'*
> *Oh, how the people cheered at that; such cheers were never heard.*
> *They got the word, a hundred helped, and soon the boat was manned,*
> *Five thousand eager, wistful eyes keen-watching from the land.*
> *A shout! What's that? From lip to lip the glorious message goes —*
> *'She's launched — she's safe,' and cheer on cheer to highest Heaven rose.*
>
> *Yes, sir, they reached the wreck all right and brought her crew to shore;*
> *They only did their duty, sir, as men, and nothing more.*
> *But if you ever hear folk sneer at fishermen I wish*
> *You'd tell them straight we can, if needs, do other things than fish*
> *And if they ask for proof just tell how Folkestone's lads went forth*
> *At duty's call, without a fear, and faced a sea of wrath,*
> *How in November, ninety-one, in fiercest gale that blew,*
> *They launched the boat and brought to land that luckless vessel's crew.*

Reprinted from the Folkestone 'Visitors List and Society Journal.'

The wreck of the *Benvenue* as it appeared in daylight. At the first attempt at launching, the Hythe lifeboat capsized with one crew member being drowned. Five were lost from the crew of the sailing ship, including Captain Moddrell, who was trapped in his cabin. A special Silver Medal commemorating the rescue was minted and awarded to all thirty-four involved in the various attempts from the shore. Just under five years later the sailing vessels *Agdar* and *Baron Holberg* were to become total wrecks on this same stretch of the coast.

The wreck of the 273-ton Norwegian barque *Leif* just to the east of Dover Harbour on 14 November 1894 completes this series of sailing vessel casualties. In storm conditions the *Leif* made for Dover Bay, but instead struck the pier and drove ashore stern-first under the cliffs. Her master was drowned but the seven crewmen were rescued by the coastguards using their rocket apparatus.

Above: Steamships have also had their fair share of disasters. Sometimes they were deliberately put ashore to prevent them from sinking after a collision. The reason for the presence of the Grove Line steamer *Boxgrove* on Deal beach in this photograph is not known. Neither is the date, but it is probably during the first decade of the twentieth century. (W.H. Franklin)

Opposite below, right and below: The stranding of the Brocklebank steamer *Mahratta* at Easter in 1909 became one of the most notorious wrecks on the Goodwin Sands. Shortly after her master realized he was aground he found that the chief engineer had committed suicide, not due to the fate of the ship but as a result of a domestic problem he could not face.

Although a number of tugs were employed, the *Mahratta* could not be extracted from the grip of the Sands and she soon broke in two. Most of her valuable cargo of tea was, however, recovered, a fair part of which was smuggled ashore and hidden in many places out of sight of the Revenue men. Visits by boatmen in small boats were frequent, as shown in the photograph to the right, for the locals had not lost their interest in contraband of earlier years.

Below, a closer view shows the partially flooded main deck of the stranded *Mahratta*. By a remarkable coincidence her successor in the Brocklebank fleet was lost only a short distance away in September 1939. (Louis G. Carpenter)

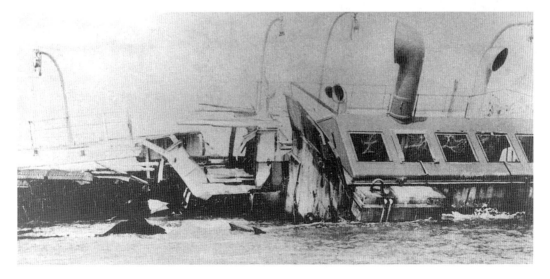

Arguably the most famous relatively recent wreck on the mainland was the five-mast German full-rigged ship *Preussen*, which drove aground near the South Foreland after colliding with the railway steamer *Brighton* off Newhaven. The date was 6 November 1910. This magnificent vessel would have survived had not a gale developed as she made her way back up the Channel to Dover for repairs.

The master of the steamer *Brighton* misjudged the speed of the *Preussen* as he cut across the latter's bows. At 1,100 grt, this crack turbine-driven ship on the Newhaven-Dieppe crossing was only one fifth the size of the sailing ship, which was exceeded in size by only three others in the history of sail.

The dismantling of the *Preussen* continued until the outbreak of the First World War. This view from aloft shows the size of one of the lower yards, each of which was 102ft in length. Originally, the ship could set thirty square sails and eighteen fore and aft sails, comprising in total 59,000 square feet of canvas. (Dover Museum)

In the days following the stranding of the *Preussen*, twelve tugs of several nationalities struggled to save her, but the continuing gales frustrated their attempts and eventually they had to give up. The two passengers and all the crew remained aboard for three days while these efforts were made. At high tide the wreck was almost covered by broken water. (Whorwell, Dover)

The remains of the centre part of the ship as they appear today on a very low tide. The west-facing bow is also recognizable and other residual ribs and steelwork still give an impression of the original 433ft length of the *Preussen*. (A.L.)

The view of the cliffs from near the site of the *Preussen* wreck. It lies directly offshore from a cut in the cliffs for a hoist. This may already have been there, for these hoists were often used to haul up seaweed and perhaps more valuable commodities on certain dark nights. In any case it was very convenient for bringing some of the cargo ashore. (A.L.)

An example of a smaller sailing vessel driven ashore in a gale. The 60-ton Portuguese schooner *Flores* became a total wreck at Walmer on 12 January 1911. Another success was achieved by the coastguards, who saved the four crewmen by means of rocket apparatus and breeches buoy. The general cargo of the ship contained a number of chamber pots, which graced the shore for a time before the whole cargo was put up, as usual, for auction.

Some of the wrecks were broken up where they lay, others sank to some extent in the sand. This embedded hull, reminiscent of the *Amsterdam*, is one of three 40-80ft wooden ships which lie at the low tide limit in Sandwich Bay, opposite the old clubhouse of the Prince's Golf Course. They may have been victims of the same storm in November 1877 that caused the wreck of the *Star of the Ocean*. (A.L.)

A similar wreck to the *Flores*, the 75-grt Salcombe ketch *Kate* lies aground after striking the chalk ledge near Newgate Gap in the cliffs at Margate on 12 April 1913. Her crew got ashore in their own boat. She had a different cargo: cement and whitening, which she was carrying from Cliffe Creek to Plymouth. Hardened bags of cement remained on the shore for many years. (Arthur Campany)

The schooner *Robert Morris* of Caernarvon lies stranded on Deal beach on New Year's Eve 1913. Both crew and vessel were saved with the aid of the Ramsgate and Dover tugs but the ship became a victim of a German submarine in 1917. (*Dover Express*)

Ships did not only strand on the coastline or offshore sandbanks. In September 1916, the British steamer *Araby* had the misfortune to block Boulogne Harbour. She had earlier run aground outside while trying to escape from a German submarine and the accident occurred while tugs were towing the disabled vessel into port. (*Shipping Wonders of the World*)

A major salvage effort was required to raise the two halves of the *Araby*, it taking some months for the cargo to be removed and concrete patches to be secured amidships. On 11 January 1917 the two halves of the *Araby* were finally beached well clear of the fairway. Another *Araby*, this time a Royal Mail Line vessel, was sunk by mine in the gateway to the Thames barrage off Sheerness on 27 November 1940. (*Shipping Wonders of the World*)

After the First World War, steam propulsion gained rapidly over sail but wrecks of the latter still occurred. The Finnish schooner *Kaleva* was lost on the beach at the top of Exchange Street, Deal, in a gale on 11 November 1921. Her timbers and fittings were sold at auction for a mere £50.

Cross-Channel ferries suffered strandings only very infrequently, but one unlucky vessel was the French *Le Nord*, which ran ashore in fog near the South Foreland in May 1923. Built in 1898, the ship enjoyed a long but eventful career, which included ramming and sinking the Pier Works lightship at Dover in November 1901. After this grounding in 1923, she was withdrawn from service and scrapped. (World Ship Society)

Over the years Thames spritsail barges stranded on numerous occasions and usually survived. These hard-working craft were so abundant, however, that losses were inevitable. The *Thyra*, shown here at Walpole Bay, Cliftonville, in late November 1933, was one that refloated safely after her ordeal. In contrast, the total wreck of the *Vera* on the Maplin Sand on 7 November 1952 brought a Silver Medal for Margate lifeboat coxswain Denis Price for saving her crew of two from a watery grave.

In most kinds of major maritime incidents, tugs are summoned to give assistance and they have saved many ships from ultimate disaster over the years. Two examples of such aid are given on this page. Here the 3,400-grt Panamanian steamer *Alba* is assisted off the north Goodwin Sands by a Watkins tug on 17 April 1940. At left is the Dover tug *Dapper*. In total, six tugs were employed. (Arthur Taylor)

The smaller Dutch coaster *Urmajo* receives assistance from the Gamecock tug *Ocean Cock* on 18 May 1955. After also grounding on the Goodwins, the Dutch vessel was successfully refloated and taken into Ramsgate Harbour. (*East Kent Times*)

Above: After the Second World War numerous wrecks occurred on the Goodwin Sands, gaining it the name used for the title of this book. Most famous was the American Liberty ship *Helena Modjeska*, which was laden with everything from food and clothing to trucks and bulldozers. This wreck, which occurred on 12 September 1946, was much welcomed by local inhabitants as the unofficial food supplies it provided helped greatly during the harsh period of rationing. (Geoff Michell collection)

Below: Both halves of the *Helena Modjeska* were eventually refloated and the stern part was beached opposite the Guilford Hotel in Sandwich Bay, where the remainder of the cargo was unloaded, including an unexpected forty tons of unstable gelignite. The wartime beach defences were still in place in the autumn of 1946. (Geoff Michell collection)

Above: Another American vessel, the 7,600-grt *North Eastern Victory*, drove ashore on the inside of the Goodwin Sands on Christmas Eve 1946. However, there were no presents for the locals this time, for the ship soon broke in two in the bad weather and the holds flooded quickly.

Below: After a few months only the masts of the *North Eastern Victory* remained above water. These remained visible from Deal for many years but no trace of the ship can be seen today. (Fotoflite, Ashford)

Another Liberty ship, the Greek *Ira* suffered a similar fate on 8 March 1947. The coal-laden vessel at first appeared remarkably sound, but within two days it had broken in two parts just like the *North Eastern Victory*. In the background lies the wreck of the *Luray Victory* dating from 30 January 1946.

Stranded Liberty ships often broke in half just forward of the bridge if they were not refloated quickly. A further vessel of this type, the *Costas Michalos*, grounded on Banc les Quenocs west of Calais in bad weather on 26 October 1962, while on a voyage from Archangel to Calais with wood pulp. She remained there for some years before being dismantled. (Jacques Kohl)

A Goodwin Sands victim on 2 January 1948, the Italian *Silvia Onorato* seemed so secure and liable to refloat that for several days the crew refused to leave her. Eventually a forecast of bad weather and the encouragement of coxswain Fred Upton of the Walmer lifeboat persuaded them to leave. He gained the Silver Medal from the RNLI for this complicated rescue.

In the days of less powerful tugs it was often difficult to cheat the Goodwins of their prey. This is how the *Silvia Onorato* appeared a few years later. She lies in position: Lat. 51° 12' 53" N; Long. 01° 33' 04" E. (Fotoflite, Ashford)

The last commercial vessel to be wrecked at the 'Calamity Corner' of the Goodwins was the French freighter *Agen*, which drove ashore on 13 January 1952 and rapidly broke in two. Her cargo of hardwood logs drifted about the Straits for weeks. The crew were all saved by the Walmer lifeboat in another epic rescue by Fred Upton, which gained him a second Silver Medal and mechanic Percy Cavell a second Bronze. (Fotoflite, Ashford)

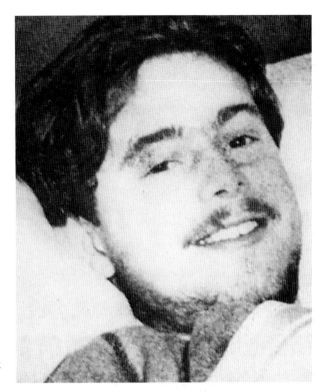

Last of all – and most tragic – was the loss of the South Goodwin lightvessel with all seven crew in the near hurricane conditions of 27 November 1954. Having broken away from her mooring, the vessel drifted rapidly north-eastwards only to strike the sandbank it guarded just south of the Kellet Gut. The only survivor, Ronald Murton, was a naturalist working for the Ministry of Agriculture and Fisheries. He was taken off just after daylight by a helicopter from the US airbase at Manston, having suffered exposure for around seven hours on the deck of the ship in atrocious conditions.

Lightvessel No.90 lies on the Goodwin Sands. In striking them she heeled over so violently that the topmasts were bent. It was to her port side rails that Murton clung through the height of the storm.

The South Goodwin lightvessel was repeatedly covered at each high tide and the gale conditions that continued prevented any further rescue attempt until after all hope had been given up for the survival of the crew. (Fotoflite, Ashford)

Above and below: Two further examples of vessels ashore on the Sands in later years. Above is the trawler *Ross Tarifa*, which broke away while under tow for breaking up in 1968, the Goodwins denying the ship dismantlers their opportunity. (John G. Callis) The vessel below typifies those of the large number that survived the sands. The Greek-registered *Neni* lies almost high and dry in calm conditions, probably in 1972. Her lines betray her British origin, for she was built originally as the *Ardglen* in 1953. She refloated safely and continued her voyage. (Chris Fright)

It was not only the offshore sandbanks that caused major casualties. The river Thames over the years has seen more collisions than groundings, but on one occasion in the fifties, the Shaw Savill liner *Corinthic* ran ashore on Stone Ness near to the position of the Dartford Bridge today. She was successfully refloated by a number of the London tugs. (*PLA Magazine*)

Even local boatmen can be caught out on occasion. The crew of the Margate pilot boat were used to putting to sea in almost all weathers, but on a dark night in February 1969 the boat was left unattended for just a few minutes. It took only that time for a sudden violent squall to break the moorings of the *Nayland* at the end of Margate jetty. The sea then carried it around the end of the stone pier and drove it ashore on the beach near the clock tower. (*Isle of Thanet Gazette*)

Moving further westwards, the shores around Eastbourne and Beachy Head have seen their share of casualties. The Greek steamer *Germania* was originally a victim of a collision on 26 April 1955 with the SS *Maro*. Going to anchor for examination, she accidentally grounded in fog east of Beachy Head lighthouse and broke her back. She was eventually refloated in February 1956 and towed to Rotterdam. (Fotoflite, Ashford)

The stranding of the 2,000-grt *Athina B* at Brighton on 21 January 1980 was witnessed by many as she came ashore between the pier and the marina. Gale to storm conditions prevailed at the time, but eventually all her crew were saved by the Shoreham lifeboat whose coxswain, Kenneth Voice, received a Silver Medal. After being refloated, the *Athina B* was towed to the river Medway for demolition. (John G. Callis)

Most recent and tragic of the major wrecks was that of the *Herald of Free Enterprise* which once more put the port of Zeebrugge on the newspaper headlines. Leaving the port with her bow doors open, the ferry capsized to land on her side on a sandbank on 6 March 1987.

The capsize of the *Herald*, resulting in the loss of 193 lives, was the greatest British maritime tragedy for many years. The Dutch salvage firm of Smit-Tak raised the vessel on 27 April 1987 and, after survey, it was towed away to be scrapped in Taiwan. (Fotoflite, Ashford)

There was fortunately very little loss of life associated with the hurricane of 16 October 1987. One serious casualty was the *Sumnia*, which struck the Admiralty pier at Dover Harbour and capsized and sank at the height of the storm. Amazingly, only two of the crew were lost, the other three being snatched from the turmoil of 20ft seas by the Dover lifeboat. (World Ship Society)

Acting coxswain Roy Couzens was awarded the RNLI Silver Medal for his courageous action and his other six crewmembers all received Bronze medals. The Smit-Tak Company also later lifted the two halves of the wreck of the *Sumnia*, which until only a few weeks earlier had been named *Summity*. It was a strange coincidence that a later *Summity* should be wrecked so near to where her namesake was beached during the war. (Fotoflite, Ashford)

Strandings of ferries are fortunately rare events, but the October 1987 hurricane caused sea conditions and wind speeds beyond anything experienced locally for many years. At Folkestone the Sealink ferry *Hengist* attempted to put to sea but rolled so much on leaving the harbour that her engines stopped due to the fuel pumps cutting out. She drifted ashore near Copt Point with only the crew aboard and they were able to reach the shore safely. (*Folkestone Herald*)

More recently, the *Stena Challenger* made an unscheduled visit to the beach just outside Calais Harbour on 20 September 1995. Local people flocked to see this unusual spectacle. The ship, 250 passengers and the crew spent twenty-three hours ashore before being refloated by Calais tugs. (Mike Jackson)

five

Fires Aboard Ship

Fires aboard ships are often serious because they can isolate passengers and crew from their means of escape to safety. The 7,118-grt Hamburg-America liner *Patria* caught fire off the Goodwins on 15 November 1899 during a homeward passage from New York. In this instance all were safely taken off by the SS *Athesia* of the same company, but the burnt-out *Patria* foundered off Deal while in tow.

Another important ship to suffer a serious fire was the cross-Channel steamer *Onward*, seen here leaving Boulogne in peacetime. The ship capsized as a result of the conflagration in Folkestone Harbour in late 1918, while acting in the role of troopship. (Louis Levi)

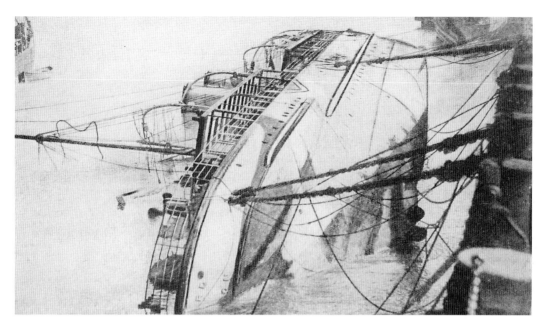

The sunken *Onward* greatly affected the working of the port and an Admiralty salvage team was called upon to remove the ship as quickly as possible. Raising the turbine steamer proved to be a difficult task. A similar fire broke out on the Danish ferry *Kronprins Frederik* at Harwich on 19 April 1953, and she also capsized alongside the berth. (*Shipping Wonders of the World*)

Eventually, a series of railway steam locomotives was harnessed to the wreck of the *Onward* and these, combined with a lifting lighter alongside, brought the vessel upright. The *Onward* was afterwards refurbished and sold to the Isle of Man SP company to become the *Mona's Isle*. She served with them up until 1947. (*Shipping Wonders of the World*)

A number of freighters have suffered fires in their cargo in the Narrow Seas. The SS *Falcon* of the General Steam Navigation Company was carrying a cargo of hemp and matches, which proved a hazardous mixture. Blazing from stem to stern, she drifted in under the cliffs of Langdon Bay, Dover, on 24 October 1926. (Robin Craig)

The 675-grt iron-screw steamer *Falcon* was built in 1876. Her bottom plates and some ribs remain to this day below the cliff ladder at Langdon Bay, a seemingly indestructible testament to the quality of the material used in her construction. (A.L.)

A cargo fire also destroyed the Pakistani steamer *Yousuf Baksh* on 8 May 1965. Carrying cotton, jute and oil cake from Chittagong to Boulogne, the vessel arrived off Dover with the jute cargo afire in her 'tween decks. As the fire spread gradually to engulf the whole ship she was beached off Deal, as shown here. Some twenty firemen of the Kent Fire Brigade were put aboard by helicopter to fight the fire. (John G. Callis)

A fire which broke out in the engine room of the Greek motor ship *Johs. P* on 18 March 1973 later spread to engulf the whole superstructure. All twenty-nine aboard were taken off safely by the Dover tug *Dominant*, a helicopter and the Dover lifeboat. Afterwards, the fire-ravaged ship was towed to Antwerp. (Fotoflite, Ashford)

Oil-tanker fires posed the greatest threat both to those aboard and those who fought them. The Swedish tanker *Johannishus* suffered a major explosion and fire after colliding with the freighter *Buccaneer* on 9 June 1955 east of Ramsgate. Almost half of the crew of forty-two were lost in this drama, which literally allowed the survivors only seconds to escape before the raging fire engulfed the whole ship. (Fotoflite, Ashford)

A similar catastrophe overtook the Norwegian tanker *Erling Borthen* when she was in collision with the Liberian steamer *Santa Rosa* three miles south of the Royal Sovereign lightvessel on 5 May 1956. Fortunately, only one man was lost on this occasion. The London coaster *Harbrook* brought thirty-six survivors to Dover. (Fotoflite, Ashford)

Last in this trilogy of tanker disasters comes the 16,000-grt Norwegian *Sitakund*. This time there was no collision and the vessel was in ballast. When passing Beachy Head on 20 October 1968 the *Sitakund* suffered three huge internal explosions and again was abandoned in flames by her crew, three of whom were lost. The blazing wreck was towed inshore to ground for a while off Eastbourne promenade, near where this picture was taken. After months ashore near Beachy Head, the two parts of the ship were towed away for scrapping.

A smaller vessel on fire is given assistance at close quarters. The German *Eleonora H* caught fire on 16 October 1974 just south of the East Goodwin lightvessel, suffering two of her five crew killed and another injured. The vessel was carrying 700 tons of sugar. In this view, men from the tug *Hibernia* and cargo vessel *Frendo Spirit* fight the fire while the Walmer lifeboat stands by. (Aeromarine, Manston)

On a larger scale, the 50,000-grt container ship *Ever Decent* was left with a fierce fire in her cargo of containers after being struck by the cruise ship *Norwegian Dream*. This dramatic incident occurred near to the Foxtrot 3 lightvessel at the northern end of the Channel separation zone in August 1999. Fortunately, this time there were no casualties. (Maritime and Coastguard Agency, Crown Copyright)

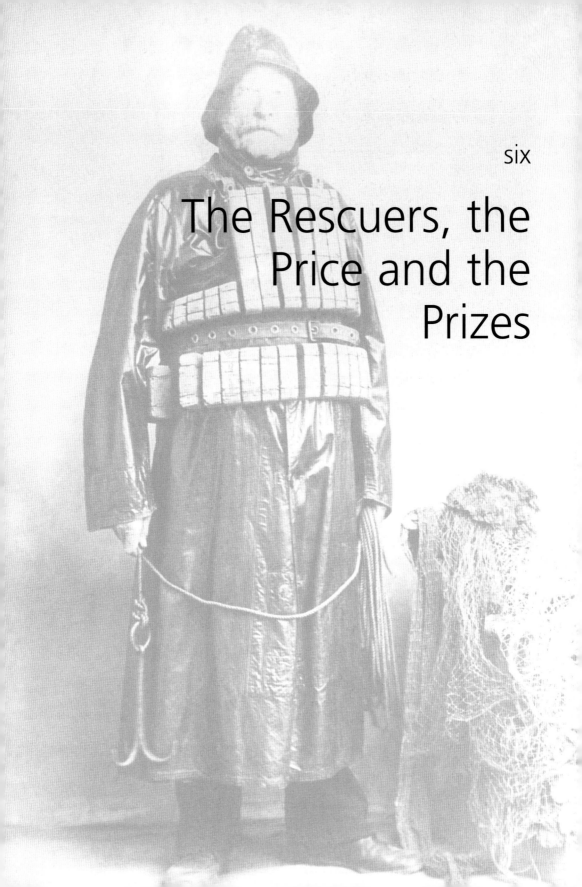

six

The Rescuers, the Price and the Prizes

Melancholy Occurrence.

Margate, March 24th, 1821.

By the Loss of the QUEEN Galley in the afternoon of *Thursday* last, the whole of the Crew consisting of the Seven following Men most unfortunately perished.----

JARVIS HOLNESS, aged **29** years, has left a Wife and **2** Infants.

DANIEL POUND aged **26** years, has left a Wife and **2** Infants.

HENRY POUND, aged **25** years, has left a Wife and **2** Infants.

JAMES WOODWARD, aged **25** years, has left a Wife.

WILLIAM RANDALL, aged **24** years, has left a Wife now pregnant, and **1** Infant.

ROBERT MAXTED, aged **24** years, } neither of them
GEORGE HARMAN, aged **23** years, } married.

With a view of alleviating the Distresses of the Surviving Relatives in several respects are very great, the Contributions of the Affluent and Charitable are earnestly entreated, and the appropriation of the Sums subscribed will be at the discretion of such of the Subscribers as may be pleased to meet for this kind purpose at the Town-Hall, on TUESDAY the 1st of May, precisely at noon.

Subscriptions will be received at the Bank, and at the several Libraries.

DENNE, PRINTER AND BOOKSELLER, QUEEN STREET, MARGATE.

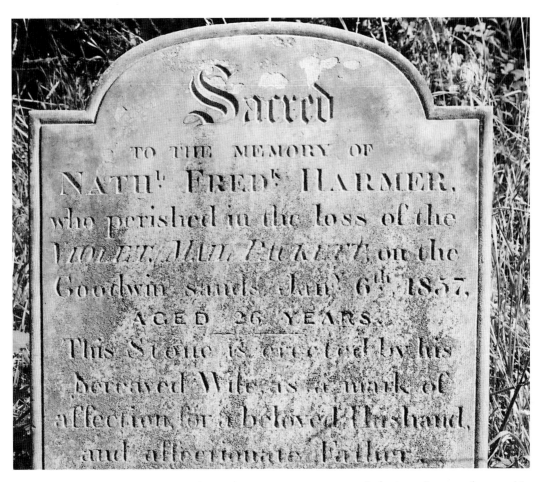

Above: A headstone to a grave in Cowgate Cemetery, Dover records the loss of twenty-six-year-old Nathaniel Harmer and the cross-Channel steam packet *Violet* on 6 January 1857 on the Goodwin Sands in a violent storm. This 292-grt ship was on the long crossing from Ostend at night when she was lost with all hands. It is remarkable that such small ships were making the crossing in all weathers in those days. A well-known Dover resident, Lilian Kay, owes her existence to the fact that her grandfather, Thomas Kay, the ship's carpenter, was unable to make this passage due to excessive consumption of alcohol. (A.L.)

Opposite: A poster requesting charitable donations for those bereaved in the shipwreck of a local galley, the *Queen*. There were no social services to support dependents in those days and such donations were extremely important. Boatmen often took chances in their calling in general and particularly in pursuit of salvage. Not infrequently these exploits cost them their lives. (Margate Museum)

Another victim of that same 1857 storm was the American ship *Northern Belle*, wrecked on the rocks at Kingsgate, near Broadstairs. The private lifeboats *Mary White* and *Culmer White* were brought overland from Broadstairs to launch from the foot of the old Smuggler's Gap. This painting by an American artist recalls something of the drama as the boat was launched into the stormy sea. (Margate Museum)

An artist's impression of conditions near to the wreck. These were particularly bad when the wind was onshore and the sea was shallow. In spite of this weather, the Broadstairs boatmen were able to take all the crew off in three attempts with no loss of life. (T. Cooper Sr)

The survivors of the *Northern Belle* were brought to the local, the Captain Digby Inn, where the second mate of the lost ship thanked the Broadstairs boatmen for their rescue. (*Illustrated London News*)

Crowds welcomed the lifeboat *Mary White* and her crew back to Broadstairs after the service to the *Northern Belle*. The crews of the two boats had rescued twenty-three men in total, five of whom had been put aboard by the Margate lugger *Ocean*. (*Illustrated London News*)

This tablet is erected to commemorate the disastrous loss of the
Victory
lugger of this port in the destructive gale of the 5th January
1857, when in a heavy and dangerous sea and before the break
of day, our boatmen, with their usual intrepidity, put out to
succour ships in distress.

The *Victory*, while sailing in the direction of the American
ship *Northern Belle*, of 1,100 tons burthen, from New York,
seen to be in imminent peril and which afterwards stranded on
the Foreness Rock, was caught in a fearful gale and plunged
down in an instant with all her crew.

The sufferers were:
John Smith, aged 63 years; William Emptage,
aged 52; Isaac Solly, aged 46; Abraham Busbridge, aged 35;
Charles Fuller, aged 34; John Emptage, aged 29; George Smith,
aged 29; Henry Paramor, aged 27; Frederick Bath, aged 22.

Such a calamity as this is not known to have occurred here before;
may never such occur again.

This tablet is also intended as a graceful tribute to the bene-
volence of persons, not only in this town and neighbourhood,
but in London and other distant places, who have so generously
responded to the public appeal made on behalf of the widows
and orphans and have by subscription amounting to two thousand
one hundred pounds declared their sympathy with a class of men
engaged in a most important, but adventurous avocation.
'Who so is wise will ponder these things.'

The celebration of the rescue of the American seamen from the *Northern Belle* was moderated considerably by the loss of all nine crew from the Margate lugger *Victory* which also went to her assistance. A similar tragedy was to occur just over forty years later when the Margate surf-lifeboat was capsized with the loss of nine men while going to the assistance of the sailing ship *Persian Empire*.

The shore at Kingsgate from where the Broadstairs lifeboats were launched to rescue the crew of the *Northern Belle*. After being brought overland, they descended the old Smuggler's Gapway (centre right) to reach the beach. This coastline of chalk cliffs with caves let into their faces and surmounted by strange flint buildings still creates a vivid impression of the smugglers' world of 200 years ago. (A.L.)

Above left: The later Broadstairs lifeboat *Christopher Waud, Bradford* with her crew on the slipway, which has long since disappeared. This 6-ton 13-cwt, self-righting boat was stationed at Broadstairs from 1888 to 1896, when it was broken up.

Above right: William 'Shah' Hiller was second coxswain of the last Broadstairs lifeboat *Francis Forbes Barton*. This picture was taken in 1939.

The crew of the *Francis Forbes Barton* strike a pose for the photographer dressed in their cork lifejackets, sou'westers and oilskins. Broadstairs lifeboat station closed in 1912. (RNLI)

Ramsgate lifeboat made many famous rescues during the
nineteenth century. This engraving depicts the saving of the crew
from the Danish barque *Aurora Borealis*. The vessel had run ashore on the
south-east spit of the Goodwin Sands on 5 January 1867. Later the wreck refloated
and drifted into the Downs. It was towed ashore for auction.

The Kingsdown lifeboat *Sabrina* drawn up on the beach with her crew. Such subjects were very popular in late Victorian times. This boat was on station near Deal from 1866 to 1871, when it was moved to Newquay. (Attributed to W.H. Franklin)

This final view of a lifeboat and crew shows the Walmer boat *Civil Service No.4* outside the boathouse, which still exists to this day. (Deal Museum)

As already recorded, the most notable of the Ramsgate rescues was that of the crew of the *Indian Chief* in January 1881. Besides receiving the RNLI Silver Medals, the crews of both lifeboat and tug all received the specially minted 'Indian Chief' medal shown here. (Ramsgate Maritime Museum)

Ramsgate lifeboat was very dependent on the harbour steam-tug to tow it quickly to any casualty. It comes as no surprise, therefore, that the crews of the *Aid* and *Vulcan* shared in the numerous medals awarded by the RNLI. Captain Daniel Reading, master of the tug *Vulcan*, gained the Silver Medal for helping to save the crew of eight from the Sunderland brig *Defender* which had stranded on the Goodwin Sands on 19 March 1872. (Ramsgate Maritime Museum)

Left and below: Thomas Nicholls was a seaman aboard the tug *Aid* that towed the Ramsgate lifeboat *Northumberland* to the 170-grt Spanish brigantine *Samaritano* wrecked on the Margate Sand in 1860. He and the other members of his crew, Daniel Reading (master), J. Simpson (mate), J. Denton, J. Freeman, T. Larkins, W. Penman, W. Matson and W. Solly, were awarded the Board of Trade medal, the sum of £2 and bibles with the inscription below. (Ramsgate Maritime Museum)

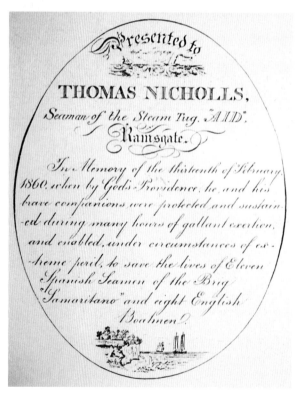

Presented to

THOMAS NICHOLLS,

Seaman of the Steam Tug "AID",

Ramsgate.

In Memory of the thirteenth of February 1860, when by God's Providence, he, and his brave companions were protected and sustained during many hours of gallant exertion, and enabled, under circumstances of extreme peril, to save the lives of Eleven Spanish Seamen of the Brig "Samaritano" and eight English Boatmen.

In addition, coxswain James Hogben and the crews of the lifeboat and tug *Aid* were each awarded a medal by Queen Isabella II of Spain, a certificate and the sum of £3. James Hogben's certificate, roughly translated, reads, 'He has been decorated with a gold medal for his help and bravery in risking his life to assist the Spanish brigantine *Samaritano* shipwrecked on the bank off Margate on 3 February 1860.' (Ramsgate Maritime Museum)

The rest of the crew members of the tug and lifeboat received this Silver Medal, which shows the head of Queen Isabella II on the reverse. (Ramsgate Maritime Museum)

The Board of Trade Medal was awarded to all who helped to rescue those aboard the *Samaritano,* who comprised eleven Spaniards, six Margate boatmen and two Whitstable fishermen. This medal was presented to Robert Solly, one of the crew of the lifeboat *Northumberland*. (Frank Boxall)

Two different harbour tugs from a slightly later period. Illustrated above is the 950 IHP paddle tug *Aid (II)* constructed in 1889, which worked at Ramsgate until the First World War. Her powerful engines and pumps were able to save many vessels, including the French fishing boat shown here.

The Dover Harbour Board 366-grt screw tug *Lady Crundall* was built at the still later date of 1906. A major asset to the harbour, she was much larger than the *Aid (II)* and achieved 1,500 IHP on trials. Having been taken over for naval service in the First World War, she was sold abroad directly afterwards. *Lady Crundall* was one of the tugs that saved HMS *Sappho* from sinking (*q.v.*).

An account of the rescue of two men from the Dutch sloop *Helena* by the Dunkirk lifeboat *Susan Gray* on 30 October 1887:

A real hurricane was unleashed on our coastline at around four in the morning. It was to be a fatal and unforgettable day.

At 8.30 a.m. it was learned from the three cannon shots fired from the signal station that a ship was in distress to the east of the port. It was the Dutch sloop Helena, *Captain Pluckthie, on a voyage from Portsmouth to Dunkirk with a mineral cargo. After losing all sails and facing other trials, the vessel, out of control and driven by the wind, came ashore a short distance from the battery of Fort Lefrinckoucke, remaining about fifty metres seaward of the dunes.*

In response, the crew of the lifeboat Susan Gray *was soon mustered, coxswain Noedts taking command, and they left immediately, hauled by the tug* Rapide, *Captain Lacroix, to face a stormy, raging sea which broke constantly in fury over and beneath their boat. Enormous waves slowed the tug, but it succeeded eventually in reaching deep water although, in passing over the bar, the boat was lifted on a huge wave and second coxswain Marquette was struck on the head by the anchor, receiving a serious injury to his eye.*

All attempts to approach the Helena, *however, proved fruitless and no signal being made from the ship, coxswain Noedts, believing that the crew had already reached land, decided to return to station, where the boat arrived at about 11.30 a.m.*

Subsequently, information reached the port at 12.15 p.m. by runner from Lefrinckoucke that the crew of the Helena *was still aboard and had now taken refuge in the rigging. The* Susan Gray *immediately left again, towed this time by the tug* Dunkerquois, *Captain Charet, with the same crew except for second coxswain Marquette and crewman Pierre Eggrycke, who had been so affected by the cold as to be unable to make another trip. These indefatigable boatmen were this time determined to accomplish their task.*

The newspaper *Phare de Dunkerque* of 1 November 1887 gave the following account:

At the first news of the disaster, a large crowd gathered on the coast, about forty of which tried to organize help, enquiring which means of saving life were available, encouraging those shipwrecked and giving them advice on how to secure the line for a breeches buoy. However, this latter route was impracticable because the sloop was almost completely submerged and the poor people aboard could find nowhere to secure a line.

Some time after the tug Rapide *had been spotted the small ship's boat of the* Helena *was washed ashore on the beach, whereupon several men of good intent seized it and dragged it with much effort about 400 metres upwind of the wreck.*

Three of them, having courage above most, took their places in it. They were Henri Versaille, Hivin, son of one of our lifeboat men, and William Muray. But they possessed only two inferior oars and, seeing the state of the sea, they had difficulty in keeping the boat's head to wind. These three courageous men fought vigorously against the violence of the seas without success, for, having arrived at a point twenty metres from the sloop, their boat was caught by a wave and thrown heavily on to the shore, allowing them time only to dive into the sea and swim to dry land.

During this time, continuous cries for help were heard and not one of those who attended this terrible drama could hold back the tears. A woman and a man were lashed to the foot of the mast, and another, the second mate, had tied himself to the starboard shrouds. Finally, a fourth man, the pilot M. Ficquet, was likewise secured on the port side.

Scarcely had the ship's boat been stranded on the shore than the bridge of the ship was washed away, the lady attached to the mast lost her footing and was submerged. From afar the remaining crew seemed to cry, 'You see us, and yet you do not come to our aid!' Had the rope that held the poor woman carried away completely she would have been cast up on the shore; unfortunately it held and although several onlookers plunged into the foaming waters in an attempt to save her, the captain's sister drowned.

The ship's boat, carried once more by the same men, was launched a second time but again achieved nothing. At about twenty metres from the Helena it was swamped and those aboard were once more lucky to escape by swimming ashore. Only two men now remained on the wreck. They were the second mate and pilot Ficquet, who, facing this tragic calamity and, seeing the efforts of those who came to their aid brought to nought, accepted death as inevitable. 'I could have lasted no more than another half-hour,' said Ficquet. 'Me neither!' the Dutch seaman agreed afterwards.

While all this frightful drama was taking place, the lifeboat, fighting valiantly under a leaden sky against the breaking waves, which slowed its progress, was approaching the Helena. Her crew guided it as quickly as possible to the wreck, which gave new courage to those aboard, but even as they manoeuvred to throw a line, coxswain Noedts, seeing the two remaining survivors lashed to the shrouds, and recognizing one of them in horror as his brother-in-law M. Ficquet, fell senseless to the deck. It seemed that even now those left aboard the Helena were doomed to perish, but within a few moments second coxswain Gossin had taken over command of the Susan Gray, whose crew was now reduced to nine men all told – it seemed the odds of success were even more stacked against her.

The sea, meanwhile, broke ceaselessly over the wreck, burying it as a half-tide rock, surrounded by all kinds of broken rigging and general flotsam, which made their approach alongside a perilous one indeed. Nevertheless, after several attempts made with all the courage required of the occasion, they succeeded at last in throwing a line into the shrouds that the Dutch mate was able to seize. He tied it to the remaining mast where the pilot Ficquet could reach it, so that at last the two could be hauled to the safety of the boat and thus were saved from the awful fate that had threatened them.

Their torture seemed almost at an end, but by now everyone aboard the Susan Gray was exhausted and, with some of their oars broken, they faced a yet greater trial by the elements if they were to return to port. Faced with an awful dilemma, Gossin took what he considered was the only route that offered a chance of survival and allowed the sea to carry the boat on to the beach. Most of the crew moved aft in order that it would drive as far as possible up the sand, a process that was helped by those gathered there.

Once safely ashore, their successful rescue of the remaining two men was greeted with great acclaim, and the survivors and the still unconscious coxswain Noedts were speedily conveyed by carriage to the town where they were given every attention and care to alleviate their suffering. In the afternoon a further carriage brought in all the valiant lifesavers, the two coxswains receiving the greatest praise.

No one knew at what moment the sea had taken the unfortunate Dutch captain, for his disappearance had not been noted. The seaman torn away by the surf almost at the moment when the Helena struck the shore and the ship's cabin boy lashed in the rigging who swiftly came to the same end brought to four the number of victims of this disastrous shipwreck, the thought of which still leaves one frozen with horror.

Was it not a truly heartrending spectacle to see these men and this woman lashed to a ship only metres from safety, succumb, overwhelmed by the tempestuous sea in full view of an anxious crowd, who heard their cries of terror and distress carry clearly over the roar of the storm and yet could do so little to save them.

Notes: This abridged translation has been made from the book, *Du Sauvetage en Mer à Dunkerque*, by L. Mechain and M. Raffoux, published at Dunkirk in 1979.

The lifeboat *Susan Gray* had been a private gift to replace the surfboat at Margate but was rejected as unsuitable for beach work and later presented or sold to the port of Dunkirk.

The luggers, which had earlier been one of the main lifesaving craft, continued to work for many years after the introduction of the lifeboats. Deal boatmen used them to deliver anchors and generally service vessels anchored in the Downs but they also went a long away down-Channel to put pilots aboard vessels, some, like the *Walmer Castle*, being lost in the process. A memorial notice is given below. (Deal Maritime Museum)

In Affectionate Remembrance of

HENRY AXON, aged 40
DAVID AXON, aged 36
WILLIAM CUSHNEY, aged 36

JAMES HOILE, aged 38
JAMES ARNOLD, aged 32
WILLIAM GILCHRIST, aged 29

Who lost their lives by the foundering of the Deal Pilot Lugger "Walmer Castle," off Dunnose, Isle of Wight, March 15th 1892.

WE saw her beating along the coast,
  And watched her with anxious eye;
A dread in our hearts, she must be lost,
  For the sea ran mountains high.

We could see her crew, four men or five,
  And quite at their ease seemed they,
Many a gale they'd weathered alive,
  As fierce as the one that day.

Full dressed were they, for the sea washed o'er,
  Then another sail was bent,
To keep them off the terrible shore,
  Like a bird of the sea she went.

Dancing and leaping over the tide,
  Till struck by a fearful wave,
Good God! We saw her turn on her side,
  And nought could be done to save.

Brave men in their anguish strove to leap,
  To aid, through the waters black,
Victims, that's all, for the angry deep,
  But the calmer kept them back.

She drifted on with the ebbing tide,
  By our pier and homesteads bright
Stealing along on the channel wide,
  Hiding herself in the night.

But wandered back with the morrow's sun,
  A guilty murderess she,
Hovering about where the deed was done,
  A pitiful sight to see.

They'll float her again gay and new,
  Though ere long must age condemn,
She'll perish and rot—but what of her crew?
  There's glory awaiting them.

'Tis said the new life, just as it should,
  Begins where the present ends,
Men died at their post, working for good,
  And God has given them friends.

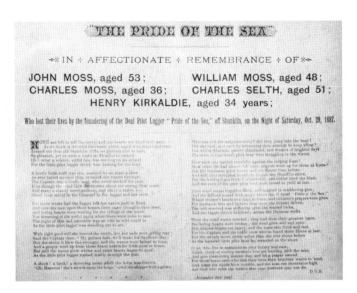

Another Deal lugger which suffered a similar fate was the *Pride of the Sea*, also lost on the Isle of Wight on 29 October 1887. (Deal Maritime Museum)

They also continued their work of saving lives for, on 21 January 1881, the Margate lugger *Secret* rescued the Dutch master, Blas Meilmeister, from the Middleburg smack *Vazchesharner*, wrecked on the Long Sand. He had been lashed to the mast for thirty hours. His remaining crew, six in number, all perished. Later he was photographed with his rescuers. The names of the others in the group are John Davies (master), John Dixon, Samuel Davis, John Sandwell, George Knott, Edward Knight and Henry Brockman. (W.M. Locke)

One of the last Deal luggers, the *Renown*, built in 1861, was broken up on Deal beach in 1909.
(Deal Maritime Museum)

Rye Harbour Lifeboat Station

The station was established in 1803 and taken over by the RNLI in 1833.

1831	Gold Medals awarded to Lt. E.C.Earle RN amd Lt. John Steane RN for trying to save the crew of the brig *Fame* wrecked 1 February. All the crew drowned but gold worth £3,000 was recovered.
1832	Gold Medal awarded to Lt. H.L.Parry RN for rescuing the master and 30 men from the French fishing boat *L'Aimee* ashore in Rye Bay on 21 November 1831.
1834	Silver Medals awarded to Lt. John Somerville RN and Lt. Richard Morgan for rescuing the master and seven men from the Dutch brig *Conrad* wrecked near Rye on 22 January. Four other men drowned.
1835	Silver Medal to Lt. William Southey RN for rescuing the master and six men from the French brig *Charles Tronde* ashore near No. 31 Tower, Rye on 9 October.
1844	Silver Medal awarded to James Bacon, master of the smack *British Rover*, for rescuing the master and 12 men from the wrecked ship *Singapore* which drove ashore at Rye on 14 July.
1864	Silver Medal awarded to William C. Buck for rescuing the master of the Jersey smack *Thetis* which, during a gale force wind, had sunk off 36 Tower, Winchelsea on 13 February.
1891	Silver Medal awarded to James Collins, Coxswain of the Rye lifeboat in acknowledgement of his gallant services in which he assisted in saving 45 lives during 12 years.
1928	The lifeboat was launched in a south-west gale to the vessel *Alice*. The lifeboat capsized during the service and the whole crew of 17 perished. The men who lost their lives were Herbert Head, Coxswain, and two sons, James and John; J. Stonham, 2nd Coxswain; H. Cutting, Bowman and his two brothers, Robert and Albert; Charles, Robert and Alexander Pope, three brothers; William and Leslie Clark, brothers; Maurice and Arthur Downey, cousins; H. Smith, W. Igglesden and C. Southerden. After the disaster the station was closed.
1966	Inshore lifeboat station established.
1981	Framed letter of appreciation signed by the Chairman to Helmsman Keith W. Downey for the rescue of three people from the 24ft ketch *Midley Belle*. The ketch was sailed into open seas by her remaining crew and eventually taken in tow by the Dungeness lifeboat.
1984	A vellum was awarded to commemorate the station's aggregate of 144 years' service covering the periods 1803 to 1928 and 1966 to 1984.
1990	150th Anniversary Vellum awarded to station.
1995	New boathouse, timber slipway and elevated walkway to the harbour constructed.
1996	Atlantic 75 class lifeboat B727 placed on station.

A brief history of Rye Harbour lifeboat station, which spans two centuries.

Rye Harbour station suffered the worst lifeboat disaster on the south-east coast, when, on 15 November 1928, all seventeen of the crew of the *Mary Stanford* were lost returning from a service to a vessel which had already got out of danger. Unfortunately, the signal to return immediately was not seen as the boat departed on her mission.

The grave of the seventeen men from the *Mary Stanford* in Rye Harbour churchyard. It was an event rendered more tragic by the number of young men who were lost from the village. (A.L.)

RYE HARBOUR LIFEBOATS

OF THE

ROYAL NATIONAL LIFE-BOAT INSTITUTION, 1852-1928.

FIRST LIFEBOAT.

				LIVES SAVED FROM SHIPWRECK
1852	August 15	Brig, "Avon," of London	::	:: 3
1862	December 10	American ship, "James Browne"	::	:: 18
1867	January 23	Barque, "Marie Amelie," of Quimper	Assisted to save vessel and	14
	February 1	Brigantine, "Estelle," of Preston	Saved vessel	::

SECOND LIFEBOAT.

The "STORM SPIRIT," out of the Solicitors' and Proctors' Lifeboat Fund.

1867	October 22	Ship, "Michael Loos," of Antwerp.	Stood by vessel	::
1869	February 14	Brig, "Pearl," of Shoreham	::	:: 8
1871	January 16	Brig,"Elizabeth & Cicely," of Guernsey	::	:: 8
	December 18	Barque, "Robina," of North Shields	::	:: 8
1874	February 25	Schooner, "Helene," of Cranz	::	:: 4
1876	January 21	Brig, "Fred Thompson," of Dundee	Stood by vessel	::
1877	December 22	Schooner, "Vier Broders," of Groningen	::	:: 4
1878	January 28	Schooner, "Fearless," of Guernsey	::	:: 6

THIRD LIFEBOAT.

The "FRANCES HARRIS," legacy of the late Mrs. Harris of Streatham.

1884	January 23	Brig, "Silksworth," of Blyth	::	:: 7
1890	December 4	Steam Tug, No.15, of Plymouth	Assisted to save vessel and	6
1891	December 28	Barque, "Warwickshire," of London.	::	:: 18
1896	December 5	S.S. "Menzaleh," of London.	Rendered assistance	::

FOURTH LIFEBOAT.

The "JOHN WILLIAM DUDLEY," legacy of the late Mr. J.W. Dudley, of Woodford.

1900	October 25	Ship, "Helicon," of Hamburg.	Rendered assistance	::
1901	January 19	Cutter, "Jeune Arthur," of Cherbourg.	::	:: 4
1902	February 23	Ketch, "Pilot," of Plymouth.	Saved vessel and	:: 4
1904	Feb. 20-25	S.S. "Lake Michigan," of Liverpool.	Stood by vessel	::
	May 2	Ship, "Derwent," of London.	Stood by vessel	::
1905	June 22	S.S. "Clara," of London	Stood by vessel	::
1907	January 22	Ketch, "Lord Tennyson," of London.	Rescued 3 and a dog	:: 3
	March 18	S.S. "Swan," of Sunderland.	Stood by vessel	::
1909	December 22	S.S. "Salatis," of Hamburg.	Rendered assistance	::
	December 22	Boat of Tug, "Oceana," of London.	::	:: 3
1910	March 9	Steam Trawler, "Margaret," of Rye.	Stood by vessel	::
1912	December 26	S.S. "Bedeburn," of Newcastle	Assisted to save vessel	::
1916	April 17	S.S. "Kirnwood," of Middlesborough.	Rendered assistance	::

FIFTH LIFEBOAT.

The "MARY STANFORD," legacy of the late Mr. John Stanford.

1920	May 28	S.S. "Thora Fredrikke," of Porsgrund.	Stood by vessel	::
1921	March 29	Barge, "Lady Ellen," of Woodbridge	::	:: 2
1923	February 2	Motor Schooner, of Falmouth	::	:: 8
	December 13	Aeroplane, G-E.B.I.J. Sperry	Salved aeroplane	::

Total 128

The 'MARY STANFORD' was launched to the help of the S.S. "Alice," of Riga on the 15th November 1928. A whole South West gale was blowing with a very heavy sea. As she was coming home, the life-boat capsized in the surf, with the loss of the whole of her crew of seventeen. The life-boat station was not re-established after the loss of the "MARY STANFORD" until 1966 when the inshore life-boat was placed on duty.

Lifeboats suffered an extra dimension of danger in wartime but relatively few were lost. Some came perilously close to it. This damage was sustained by the Newhaven lifeboat *Cecil and Lilian Philpott* when called to help HM Trawler *Avanturine* which was running ashore in a gale. Unfortunately, the trawler collided with the lifeboat. Her bowman, Ben Clark, was lost and her coxswain and three others injured but the trawler was still guided to safety. This was another exceptional service, with coxswain Leonard Peddlesden gaining the RNLI Silver Medal and the other six in the crew the Bronze. (RNLI)

A general medal awarded to those who suffered the hazards at sea in the mercantile marine in the First World War. (Frank Boxall)

Margate lifeboatmen from two different periods. George Stephen Sandwell, a fisherman, joined the lifeboat crew around 1877 and went on to serve for about fifty years. Members of the Sandwell family have been associated with the Margate lifeboat from that time until the present day. (Ken Sandwell)

Albert Joseph Scott entered the Margate boat *North Foreland* in the 1950s and served for twenty-three years, sixteen and a half of them as second mechanic. The boat rescued 264 lives during his period of service. It is interesting to compare the waterproof clothing and lifejackets from the two different periods. (RNLI)

A comparison of lifeboat services in bad weather from two different decades as portrayed by artists. This work by E.W. Cooke was painted in about 1857 and is entitled 'The Ramsgate lifeboat and pilot boat going to the assistance of an East Indiaman foundering on the North Sand Head of the Goodwin Sands'.

A drawing by William McDowell commemorating the efforts of the Walmer lifeboat and 'lifeboat surgeon' James Hall for boarding ships in all weathers during the Second World War in order to attend to sick crewmen. (*The Sphere*)

Left: This range of rescues ends with a French miscellany. In this first picture, Captain Landrau of the wrecked freighter *Agen* steps ashore from the Walmer lifeboat at Deal in January 1952 after his ordeal on the Goodwins. He was reluctant to leave even after his ship had broken in two. (Chris Fright)

Below: The crew of the Boulogne trawler *Jean Pierre et Phillippe* was cared for at the Tartar Frigate public house near Broadstairs Harbour after the vessel had been driven ashore in Viking Bay on 11 November 1962. Later they were moved to the Continental Hotel at Ramsgate, where this picture was taken. (*Isle of Thanet Gazette*)

The French Lifeboat Service Medal presented to Reginald 'Ginger' Thomas and the other crew members of the Walmer lifeboat *Charles Dibdin (Civil Service No.2)* for saving the crew of the *Agen*.

The Boulogne lifeboat made a courtesy visit to Dover for the naming ceremony of their new lifeboat *City of London (II)* on 28 May 1998. (A.L.)

Nowadays the emphasis of lifeboats is on speed, and rigid inflatables are used more and more for inshore work. The *British Diver II* is seen operating at Harwich. (A.L.)

One of the four new lifeboats now operating on the Thames. This one is seen in service at Gravesend, while a second is moored at Tower Pier. A third works from Chiswick and the other from Teddington. Note how the crew's clothing and headgear has changed greatly from that of the two men shown previously. (A.L.)

Index

Note: MV = Motor vessel; SS = Steam ship; PS = Paddle steamer

Active (West Indiaman) 11, 84
Admiral Gardner (East Indiaman) 11, 85
Adventure (HMS) 36
Afghanistan (SS) 72
Agdar 95
Agen (SS) 112, 154, 155
Aid (tug) 139-142
Ajax II (HM drifter) 26
Alba (SS) 107
Albion (East Indiaman) 11
Alert (cable ship) 42
Amsterdam (East Indiaman) 11, 84, 102
Anglia (hospital ship) 8, 9, 44
Anne (third-rate warship) 14
Araby (SS) 104
Athesia (SS) 122
Athina B (MV) 117
Aurora (troopship) 8
Aurora Borealis (barque) 136, 137
Avanturine (HM trawler) 151
Barn Hill (SS) 52
Baron Douglas (SS) 74
Baron Holberg 95
Benvenue (ship) 93-95
Benwyvis (SS) 74
Bjorgholm (MV) 73
Blackhill (SS) 50
Blackwater (HMS) 9, 18
Blanche (HMS) 9, 36
Bona Fulmar (MV) 80
Bourrasque (warship) 40
Boxgrove (SS) 96
Bradford (lifeboat) 12, 91
Brazen (HMS) 39
Brighton (SS) 8, 96
Britannia (East Indiaman) 11, 85
British Trent (MV) 10, 11
British Diver II (lifeboat) 156
Brussels (SS) 45, 46
Buccaneer (SS) 126
Bulwark (HMS) 8, 9, 21, 64
Bywell Castle (SS) 64
C-3 (HMS submarine) 34
Cambridge Ferry (MV) 78
Cap San Antonio (MV) 121
Carlisle (fourth-rate warship) 8
Cecil and Lilian Philpott (lifeboat) 151

Charles Dibdin (Civil Service No.2) (lifeboat) 155
Chasseur 9 (warship) 41
Christopher Waud, Bradford (lifeboat) 135
City of York (SS) 70
Civil Service No.4 (lifeboat) 138
Codrington (HMS) 39
Convoy CW08 losses 61
Corinthic (SS) 116
Costas Michalos (SS) 110
Culmer White (lifeboat) 132, 133
Dalryan (SS) 53
Dapper (tug) 107
Datum (HM drifter) 26
Defender (brig) 139
Deutschland (SS) 9
Dione (SS) 75
Dominant (tug) 125
Dorothy (brig) 15
Duchess of Kent (PS) 64
Dunbar Castle (MV) 9
Dunkerquois (tug) 144
Earl of Eglinton (East Indiaman) 89
Eleonora H (MV) 128
Emile Deschamps (warship) 8, 10
Empire Commerce (SS) 58
Enchantress (sloop) 90
Erling Borthen (MV) 127
Ernani (SS) 59
Ethel Everard (barge) 57
European Gateway (MV) 10, 77
Ever Decent (MV) 10, 11, 128
Falcon (SS) 11, 124
Flandres (SS) 71
Flirt (HMS) 22
Flores (schooner) 102
Floridian (emigrant ship) 8
Fluor (SS) 71
Fortitude (ship) 87, 88
Francis Forbes Barton (lifeboat) 135
Franconia (SS) 65, 66
French Dunkirk losses 40, 41, 55
French lifeboat 144, 145, 155
Frendo Spirit (MV) 128
Friedrich der Grösse (warship) 16
Friend to All Nations (lifeboat) 2, 134
Germania (SS) 83, 117
Gipsy (HMS) 27, 38

Glatton (HMS) 8, 9
Gleaner of the Sea (HM drifter) 26
Glengarry (SS) 66
Grazia (SS) 50
Grønland (SS) 61
Grösser Kürfurst (warship) 8, 16, 17
Guecho (SS) 74
Hel (MV) 80
Helena (sloop) 144, 145
Helena Modjeska (SS) 108
Hengist (MV) 120
Henry Moon (SS) 60
Herald of Free Enterprise (MV) 8, 78, 118
Hercule (tug) 55
Hero (SS) 9, 18
Hibernia (tug) 128
Hindostan (East Indiaman) 11, 84, 85
Hope (galley punt) 20
Indian Chief (barque) 12, 91, 139
Intrepid (HMS) 33, 34
Iphigenia (HMS) 33, 34
Ira (SS) 110
Jean Pierre et Phillippe (trawler) 154
Johannishus (MV) 126
Johs. P (MV) 125
Kaleva (schooner) 105
Kariba (MV) 10, 81
Kate (ketch) 103
Kayseri (SS) 11
Keith (HMS) 38
König Wilhelm (warship) 17
Korenica (SS) 74
Kronprins Frederik (MV) 11, 123
L'Adroit (warship) 40
Lady Crundall (tug) 18, 143
Lady of Brussels (SS) 46
Launch Out (HM drifter) 26
Le Nord (PS) 105
Leif (barque) 95
Lightvessel losses 59
Lightvessel No.21 76
Lightvessel No.38 59, 69, 70
Lightvessel No.90 (South Goodwin) 113, 114
Liseta 62
Lundy (HMS) 71
Luray Victory (SS) 110
Lusitania (SS) 44
Mahratta (SS) 8, 96, 97
Maloja (SS) 8, 47
Maro (SS) 117
Mary (fourth rate) 8, 15
Mary Stanford (lifeboat) 12, 148-150
Mary White (lifeboat) 132, 133
Mastiff (HMS) 9, 37, 54
Melville Castle (East Indiaman) 86

Michael C (SS) 75
Minesweeper (wood) 42
Moel Eilian (barque) 66
Moldavia (SS) 9, 47
Mona's Isle (SS) 123
Mont Louis (MV) 79
Montrose (SS) 8
N.O. Rogenaes (SS) 75
Nayland (pilot boat) 116
Newhall Hills (SS) 115
Nicola (MV) 10, 82
Niger (HMS) 20
North Eastern Victory (SS) 109, 110
Northern Belle (ship) 132-134
Northern Star 2
Northfleet (emigrant ship) 8
Northumberland (third-rate warship) 8, 15
Northumberland (lifeboat) 140, 142
Norwegian Dream (MV) 10, 11, 128
Nubian (HMS) 13, 22-25
Ocean (lugger) 133
Ocean Cock (tug) 107,
Oceana (SS) 10, 68
Olau Britannia (MV) 79
Onward (SS) 11, 122, 123
Ore Meteor (SS) 76
Paracas (SS) 10
Pas de Calais (PS) 19
Patria (SS) 122
Pavon (SS) 8, 10, 41, 56
Pelter (brig) 90
Persian Empire (ship) 134
Phobos (SS) 51
Pisagua (barque) 10, 68
Plassey (ship) 92
Pluviose (warship) 19
Pommerania (SS) 9, 10, 66
Preussen (ship) 8, 10, 98-101
Pride of the Sea (lugger) 147
Princess Alice (PS) 8, 64
Princess Irene (HMS) 8
Prins Alexander (MV) 75
Prudential (lifeboat) 73
Queen (galley) 130
Queen of the Channel (MV) 57
Rapide (tug) 144
Ravensbourne (PS) 64
Renown (lugger) 148
Restoration (third-rate warship) 8, 15
Roburn (drifter) 26
Rosa Mary 67
Sabrina (lifeboat) 138
St Eloi (MV) 78
Samaritano (brigantine) 140-142
Sandhurst (SS) 39

Santa Rosa (SS) 127
Sappho (HMS) 8, 18, 143
Sappho (SS) 8, 18, 143
Secret (lugger) 147
Silvia Onorato (SS) 111
Simon Bolivar (MV) 8, 9, 48, 49
Sirocco (warship) 41
Sitakund (MV) 127
Skyron (SS) 80
Solway Firth (SS) 71
Spaarndam (SS) 9, 49
Spanish Prince (SS) 8
Speedlink Vanguard (MV) 77
Spotless Prince (HM drifter) 26
Star of the Ocean (brig) 90, 102
Stena Challenger (MV) 11, 120
Stirling Castle (third-rate warship) 8, 11, 15
Strathclyde (SS) 65
Submarine losses 29
Summity (MV) 60, 120
Sumnia (MV) 120
Susan Gray (lifeboat) 144, 145
Suzanne (tug) 76
Takara (MV) 82
Teoatl (MV) 80
Terukuni Maru (MV) 9, 43, 47
Texaco Caribbean (MV) 10, 82
Thames lifeboat 156
The Queen (SS) 26, 46

Thetis (HMS) 33
Thyra (barge) 106
Tigress (East Indiaman) 89
Tina Primo (SS) 52
Titanic (SS) 9, 68
Torpedo Boat No.4 (HMS) 9
Tricolor (MV) 10, 81, 82
U-12 (submarine) 20
U-33 (submarine) 45
U-48 (submarine) 27, 28, 29
UB-21 (submarine) 28
Unknown wreck (sail) 102
Urmajo (MV) 107
Vazchesharner (smack) 147
Vera (barge) 106
Vicky (MV) 10, 82
Victory (lugger) 134
Violet (PS) 131
Vindictive (HMS) 9, 30-32, 35
Volante (trawler) 62
Vryheid (troopship) 8, 11, 86, 89
Vulcan (tug) 91, 139
W.A. Scholten (SS) 8, 10, 67
Walmer Castle (lugger) 146
Walpole (East Indiaman) 11
Western Farmer (SS) 73
Yousuf Baksh (SS) 11, 125
Zubian (HMS) 25
Zulu (HMS) 25

Other local titles published by Tempus

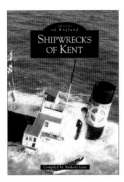

Shipwrecks of Kent
ANTHONY LANE

Kent has witnessed the passing of ships since the beginning of recorded history. The Romans landed there, and armed vessels from Spain, Holland, France and Germany have threatened its shores. This book provides a reminder of many of the more famous wrecks in the area, includes some not so familiar disasters from the past and describes some strange coincidences that have occurred over the last two centuries.
07524 1720 7

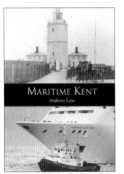

Maritime Kent
ANTHONY LANE

Maritime Kent describes the history of these different aspects of seafaring over the last two hundred years. The many photographs show how the ships have changed, and how the lives of the mariners have altered.
07524 1769 X

Guiding Lights The Design and Development of the British Lightvessel from 1732
ANTHONY LANE

Guiding Lights is the story of the lightvessels that have protected our coast since 1732 and the variety of innovative engineering that has gone into their development, from the first lighthouses and lightships, to the replacement of the bell and gong by poweful air foghorns, this book charts the methods of safeguarding vessels around the British coast.
07524 2115 8

London's River Westminster to Woolwich
CHRIS THURMAN

The river Thames has been the lifeblood of London since before Roman times. It is its *raison d'être* and has been responsible for the growth of this remarkable city. This book captures the many changes along the river over the last forty years.
07524 2595 1

If you are interested in purchasing other books published by Tempus, or in case you have difficulty finding any Tempus books in your local bookshop, you can also place orders directly through our website

www.tempus-publishing.com

or from   **BOOKPOST**, Freepost, PO Box 29, Douglas, Isle of Man, IM99 1BQ
tel 01624 836000   email bookshop@enterprise.net